Stories
of
King Arthur

Stories of King Arthur

Retold by
Blanche Winder

Illustrated

AIRMONT

AIRMONT PUBLISHING COMPANY, INC.
22 EAST 60TH STREET · NEW YORK 10022

An Airmont Classic
specially selected for the Airmont Library
from the immortal literature of the world

THE SPECIAL CONTENTS OF THIS EDITION
©, Copyright, 1968, by
Airmont Publishing Company, Inc.

ISBN: 0-8049-0167-8

Contents

Merlin	9
The White Dragon and the Red	17
The Shining Cup	27
King Mordrain's Perilous Island	35
The Fiery Star	45
The Round Table of Oak	53
The Sword in the Great White Stone	61
A Lady of the Lake	73
The Princess Guinevere	83
The Empty Seat at the Round Table	93
The Fairy Hunt	103
King Pellinore's Adventure	113
Sir Gawaine's Adventure	119
Sir Tristram's Adventure	129
The Pig-Sty Prince and the Many Travels	135
The Knight of the Sparrow-Hawk	153
The Little Prince of the Lake	163
The Wizard Bewitched	173
The Adventure of Sir Bors	181
King Arthur in the Castle Perilous	189
Sir Lancelot of the Lake	199
The Coming of Galahad	207
The Passing of the King	215

Introduction

King Arthur was the hero-chief of ancient Britain, about whom stories were told and songs were sung from the fifth century to the fifteenth, when Sir Thomas Malory wrote his great book *La Morte D'Arthur*. But Malory's book does not contain all the tales; and many of those related in this volume are taken directly from other and earlier sources. The first British historian who wrote seriously of Arthur was a Welsh bishop, Geoffrey of Monmouth. He composed, in the twelfth century, a marvelous Latin book about the King, and also about Merlin. Other books followed, mostly in French, written by poets attached to the brilliant courts of the period. An old Welsh book, which was translated in the last century by Lady Charlotte Guest, under the name of *The Mabinogion*, also contains several stories of Arthur. One of these is retold in the following pages as the *Tale of the Pig-Sty Prince*. Again, many beautiful stories are told of the mysterious cup called *The Holy Grail*, and of the adventures of Arthur's knights as they searched for that lost treasure. The loveliest of these tales were used by Tennyson in his *Idylls of the King*. If it seems strange to read of magnificent feasts and tournaments in connection with an ancient British chief, we must remember that most of the poems and stories were composed in the days of chivalry, and give us pictures of that period. A curious fact is that exactly the same tales were told in Brittany as in Wales; and Broeiliande, in the former country, is supposed to be the enchanted forest in which Merlin is now imprisoned. Many places, too, claim to be the real Avalon, the lovely island to which Arthur was taken after his last battle, and from which legend says he will one day come again. Indeed, there seems to be no end to the Arthur stories, which are contained literally in hundreds of books in English, French, and other Continental libraries.

Merlin

It was midnight. On top of a high mountain hundreds of wicked fairy-men were sitting or standing in strange shadowy groups under the tiny light of a new moon. They were talking eagerly and gloomily among themselves, and the low, deep murmur of their voices was like the sound of an angry sea. Below them were the dim houses of the villages, with many a shadowy church tower rising above the roofs. And the wicked fairy-men were saying to one another that there were too many such churches nowadays, and that every good man or good woman in the human world made the power of themselves, the spirits of evil, grow less.

A terrible-looking old wizard, with a face dark and knotted like the faces you may sometimes think you see among the tree boughs, and with a beard almost as long and gray as the long gray valley mists, spoke louder than the rest. He was as clever as he was wicked, and all the others hushed their talk to listen to him.

"What we must do," said he, "is to persuade a human maiden to marry one of us. Their children will, of course, be half-men and half-fairies. The eldest child will soon belong entirely to us, and, through him, we can regain the power in the world that we are losing so fast."

All the wicked fairy-men nodded their heads and clapped their hands. And from the valley below, they might have been a lot of ragged creaking pine trees shaking their cones together in a high wind.

"Good! Good!" they said, all together. "Very good!"

They might more truthfully have said, "Bad! Bad! Very bad!" For that was what they really meant.

The terrible old wizard glanced round the circle of dim, moonlit faces in search of one that was nice looking. But each was uglier than the last. He shook his gray head doubtfully.

"A lovely Princess lives in the castle on the opposite side of the valley," he declared. "She is the maiden I have in mind. But I do not think she would be likely to fall in love with one of *us!*"

Then a dark fairy-man stepped out from the rest. For all that he was quite one of the youngest among them, he had just kept his thousandth birthday. His long, lean hands were like birds' claws as he held them up to command attention.

"I know something of the Princess," said he. "She is a careless young thing. And now and then she goes to bed and to sleep without asking our

greatest enemies, the white spirits of the air, to protect her."

"Ah-h-h-h!" hissed all the wicked fairy-men together. "Then she puts herself in our power! Good! Good! Very good!" And, "Bad! Bad! Very bad!" went the echo of their words up to the silver stars.

The awful old wizard chuckled with delight. "Go quickly!" he cried to the young fairy-man who was a thousand years old. "Put on your bat's wings and fly to her window! If the white spirits of the air are not there, you will be able to get in, and to change yourself into anything you like!"

So the bad fairy-man fastened on his bat's wings and swept over the valley, quite hiding, for a minute, the pearly light of the moon. A jeweled lamp was set in the Princess's window, shining with a pretty golden light. But there were no white spirits hovering near. The poor little Princess had gone to bed, forgetting all about them.

So the fairy-man folded his black wings and slipped in at the open casement. And there, under the shadow of the soft silken curtains, the sweetest maiden in the world lay asleep, knowing nothing at all about her terrible visitor.

He tiptoed up to her, a dark, mysterious, cruel shadow. Then, all at once, she opened her eyes and saw him. But the good spirits were very far away, and could not show him as he really was.

And so the Princess smiled and lay looking at him. She was half dreaming; and in her dream, the old bad fairy-man seemed to be a beautiful gold-clad Prince. He lifted her in his arms, and carried her to the window sill. And then all the other wicked fairy-men came flapping about the castle on their great dark wings, so that you might have thought the roof was quite hidden by black clouds. But the little Princess was still dreaming of the beautiful Fairy Prince and of a wonderful palace, built of gold and mother-o'-pearl, where he lived with magnificently dressed courtiers to wait on him. In this dream, she married him with all the proper fairy ceremonies, and sat with him on his throne under a canopy of rubies and gold.

Night after night, the Princess dreamed this, but she always forgot all about her dream in the daytime. At last she seemed to go to sleep for a much longer time than usual, and to dream that a wonderful fairy-child was born in the gold and mother-o'-pearl palace, and that there were tremendous rejoicings all through the shining cloud-land where she and the Fairy Prince reigned as King and Queen.

Then, in her dream, there came to her for the first time the memory of the white spirits of the air. And she told the Fairy Prince, and all his courtiers, that the little baby must be christened immediately.

Behold! A great clap of thunder shook the air!

The golden light changed to darkness and the Prince and his courtiers into strange and terrible beings with wide black wings like bats. They flew hither and thither in a whirring angry crowd, and seemed to be calling to each other, "Bad! Bad! Very bad!" as they shook upon the air like storm-driven leaves. And the Princess woke in terror, to find herself quite alone, shut up in a big deserted tower, with nobody near but the fairy baby upon her knees.

She began to cry bitterly, when lo! a soft, kind little voice came from the rosy mouth of the tiny thing on her lap, which frightened her so much that she dropped the baby, but picked it up again as quickly as possible.

"Don't cry," said the little sweet baby. "I know a way to comfort and help you. And, through me, all sorts of wonderful things will come to pass."

The Princess held her little child more closely, already cheered, though still a good deal frightened, and wondering why she was shut up in a tower all by herself with the fairy baby. Then a step came up, up, up the long, winding stair, the key turned in the lock, the door opened, and a good and holy man called Blaise, who looked at her gravely but very kindly, stood on the threshold of the dreary room that was her prison.

"Oh, Blaise! Dear Blaise!" cried the poor little Princess. "What has happened?"

Blaise came up to her and put his hand on her long golden hair.

"My little Princess," said he, "it is for *you* to tell us what has happened. Strange stories are being told about you. People say that *you*—you who are a great and good King's daughter—have been, for many months, in the power of the wicked fairy-men who live on the mountain. They tell of seeing these dreadful people flying round the castle every night like enormous bats. And they declare that you have been married to one of them, secretly, and that the little baby in your arms is the son, not of a baptized human Prince, but of a Prince of wickedness and darkness, and terrible, cruel ways, like the ways of the wizards who are the enemies of men."

Then the Princess cried more bitterly than ever, and told Blaise all about it. For, at last, she remembered in the daytime the dreams of the handsome Prince, and the wonderful kingdom which he reigned over in his palace of crystal and mother-o'-pearl and gold.

"Oh, Blaise!" she sobbed. "I think it must have happened because I went to sleep without asking for the guardianship of the white spirits who love me! They went away and left me! But surely, surely, they can be brought back again!"

Then Blaise hurried off, and came back with a silver chalice full of water drawn from a well where the white spirits might often be seen flying about at sunset. And, then and there, he christened the little fairy baby—who had been listening to and understanding every word that was said—naming him Merlin. And when the water from the well sparkled in bright drops all among the baby's golden hair, little Merlin laughed and shouted with gladness, and clapped his small white hands.

"I am a human baby now!" he cried. (He could still talk quite easily, which was the only sign of the fairies left about him.) "But still I know things that other human babies will never know! And when I grow up I shall be able to use all sorts of wonderful powers that I have inherited from the fairy-men of the high mountain. But I shall use them for good, and not for evil. For, through me, a Round Table shall be given to a great King, and many knights shall sit about it, and the deeds these knights shall do will be blessed by the poor and the weak and the helpless, and sung by golden-mouthed poets for hundreds and hundreds of years!"

Then the little Princess hugged the baby even more closely, and Blaise led her down the steep, winding staircase back to her own chamber, where the white spirits who loved her flew, like snowy birds, backwards and forwards before the window, so that the wicked fairy-men of the mountain were never again able to get in.

The White Dragon and the Red

Merlin, the wonderful baby, grew up into a handsome youth, but nobody quite understood him, and a good many people were rather afraid of him. He never did naughty or cruel things, but he would often rock his sides with laughter for what seemed to be no reason at all. Sometimes he would disappear for a week or two, and it was whispered of him that he used to catch and ride the wild stags; and that, when he rode a great antlered beauty, all the pretty does and their young followed him, so that the forest glades seemed alive with flying herds of deer. The gossips said, too, that the fairy people were building a house for Merlin in the deep green places of the woods —a house with seventy windows and sixty doors, where as soon as he was old enough he would live, quite alone. But when Merlin was stared at on account of these things, he only laughed to himself, as usual, and went about his business unconcernedly.

Then, one day, a party of horsemen came riding along towards the palace in which Merlin had been born. They kept asking everybody they met where they could find a certain handsome youth of whom all sorts of strange things were said. These things were exactly the stories that were told about Merlin; so naturally everybody who answered the horsemen told them where Merlin could be found. And, sure enough, as the rider drew rein before the gate of the city, there stood the slender boy, with his laughing mouth, and eyes so clear and wild and free.

One of the horsemen sprang down, seized Merlin, and flung him on his own saddle. Then he sprang up behind, set spurs to his steed, and galloped off in company with his friends. Merlin neither struggled nor cried out. He just laughed to himself as usual; for, ever since he was a baby, he had known that this would happen to him.

On went the party of horsemen at full speed, until they came to a country far from Merlin's home. Between the mountain passes they rode, and presently came out upon a low plain, where a lot of workmen were toiling, and toiling, and toiling to build a great tower. They had brought hundreds of stones together, which were lying about broken, or piled into muddled heaps. Men on horseback rode to and fro, calling out directions, or rebuking the workmen for their carelessness. The poor workmen staggered about, placing the stones one on top of the other. But however careful they were, or in whatever posi-

The White Dragon and the Red

tion they put them, the stones were no sooner set up than they, one and all, fell down again!

Watching the work from a grassy mound stood a tall man in armour, with a crown on his head and a cruel, yet frightened face below the crown. Behind him waited a standard-bearer in royal purple. And over his crownéd head floated the flag that had floated over many a Prince of a long, long line of kings.

The company of horsemen galloped up to the mound. Taking Merlin down from the horse, they led him, bound, up to the cruel-eyed monarch who stood there.

"Is this the boy?" asked the King. "You have found the child who was described to me?"

"Yes, sire," answered the rider who had first seized Merlin. "We have found him and brought him to you."

The King looked steadily and fiercely at Merlin, who smiled quite pleasantly back at him, not at all afraid.

"You laugh, child!" said the King with a heavy frown. "You do not know your fate! Do you see those stones, and that place where men have built the foundations of a great tower?"

Merlin nodded. He looked round at the heaps of unused stones, so many of which were broken and spoiled.

"In that tower," went on the King, "I mean to

find a safe refuge from the terrible enemies who swarm round my country and who will, assuredly, ride one day over the mountains, and, unless I take the necessary precautions, conquer my kingdom, and kill me. Only a strong tower can be my haven. But even though I have tried for many months to build it, no sooner are the stones set up than they all fall down again!"

"Very likely! Very likely!" said Merlin, wise as an owl and a good deal prettier.

"Wait!" growled the King like angry thunder. "You will soon be less unconcerned. I was told by a magician that only the blood of a youth of whom it was said he was half-fairy could give firmness to the foundations of the tower. You, I understand, are that unhappy child! My tower I must have, though your blood has to be spilled in order to build it!"

Even this cruel King looked unhappy, as well as frightened, as he spoke. But for all his sorrow and fear, he was quite determined to kill Merlin, so that he could go on building his tower.

Merlin laughed, bowed, and sat himself down on the grass of the mound, right under the royal purple flag that was held by the royal purple standard-bearer.

"So? So?" said he. "But even my blood, great King, will not help you to build a tower on the top of a lake of water!"

The White Dragon and the Red

The King frowned with perplexity and stared at the boy who was half-fairy.

"Lake of water! What do you mean?" he demanded. "There is no lake here—nothing but solid, red-brown earth."

"Set your workmen to dig round the foundations of your unfinished, tumbling-down tower, and you will soon see for yourself," laughed Merlin, rocking himself to and fro, with his hands clasped about his knees.

The King—whose name was Vortigern—was so amazed that he actually did as the strange, mocking boy told him! He sent for the architect who was trying in vain to build the tower and bade him order the workmen to dig about the foundations with their spades. So the workmen stopped trying to set up the stones, and started shoveling out the soil, instead. And, behold! almost immediately they were digging in mud, and up bubbled the hidden water through the mud, and down fell the banks of the ditches, followed by all the stones that had not tumbled down before. And as the stones and banks slipped down, more and more water rushed up, till at last the whole of the middle of the plain was one great lake, from which the workmen were all running away in one direction and the architect and the horsemen in another. But King Vortigern and the fairy-child still sat together under the royal standard on the grassy summit of the mound, gazing earnestly at the enormous lake.

Then the King turned to Merlin, more afraid, now, of this strange boy than of all the people who, he expected, would come riding over the hills to kill him.

"What does it all mean?" he asked, trembling. "What does it all mean?"

Merlin shook his head. Suddenly tears sprang to his eyes and rolled down his cheeks. He was sorry for the cruel King, though Vortigern had never been sorry for *him*.

"There is a great stone below the lake," he said, in a whisper. "Two dragons sleep there—a red one and a white. One day they will come out from under the stone and meet on the waters of the lake in a fearful battle. In the white dragon is the soul of your strongest enemy—in the red dragon, Vortigern, you may see the shadow of yourself."

Then Merlin stepped down from the mound and went slowly away, and nobody tried to hold him. But Vortigern sat on the grass and stared for a week on end at the still green waters of the magical lake.

And at last, while he stared, he saw the waters shudder and shake into great waves. The waves sprang higher and higher, like horses tossing their white and shaggy manes. Then up through the hills and valleys of the storm-lashed water came the white dragon and the red. The white

dragon was as pale as snow, and the red dragon was as scarlet as blood. Their wings, high above the angry waves, looked like crimson and silver clouds flying low across the sky. And from end to end of the fairy lake, they fought each other, until, with a great cry, the red dragon fell dead upon the beach, among the green rushes and the broken stems of the water flowers.

Vortigern rose and fled. But he thought he heard the voice of the fairy-boy echoing all around about him as he went:

"In the white dragon is the soul of your strongest enemy—in the red dragon, Vortigern, you may see the shadow of yourself!"

The King reached his palace quaking with fear, but lo! his courtiers came running to tell him that the lake had sunk back deep into the earth, and that now the workmen were building his tower as fast as they could. So Vortigern began his old cruel, wicked ways once more. Then, as soon as the tower was finished, he shut himself up in it for safety. But at night, very often, he woke up panting with terror, for in his dreams he still saw the mighty battle between the white dragon and the red.

And, surely enough, one day his strongest enemy came over the hills with a great army, for Vortigern's people, racked with their King's wickedness and cruelty, had sent out a pitiful cry for help. The King who rode over the hills was great

The White Dragon and the Red

and good, and he rescued the unhappy people, and then went to the big tower and bade Vortigern come out. There was no answer from inside, and so the soldiers set fire to the tower, and it blazed fiercely for days and days, until at last the walls were all burned away and nothing was left but a heap of ruins, lying on the very spot where the red dragon had fallen dead after the great fight with the white dragon on the lake.

Vortigern had been shut up in the tower all the time, and so was killed by the great King just as the red dragon had been killed by the white. But nobody could be sorry, for had he not been cruel to everyone, and would he not have willingly slain the fairy-boy to save his own wicked life? So the good King reigned over the kingdom in his place, and was called Uther Pendragon. The reasons for this name and some of the things that he did you will read about in another story.

The Shining Cup

Long before Merlin was born, there lived in an Eastern country a good and holy man called Joseph, who had for many years been the guardian of a wonderful Cup. Nobody quite knew where his Cup had first come from, nor who had made it, nor what it was that gave it the lovely radiance which always surrounded it and made it look more beautiful than any fairy goblet set with emeralds and pearls. But all Joseph's friends knew that the Cup was a great treasure, and that only a good and faithful man could have been chosen as its guardian. So they honored and respected Joseph, and talked reverently of the precious chalice of which he had the care.

This Cup was called the Grail Cup, and sometimes Joseph would summon his children and his grandchildren (for he was quite an old man), and the best-loved of his friends, to take their seats at a silver table which he had himself made, in the middle of which he would set the Grail Cup. Then, while everybody looked at the shining mist in which the Cup was half-hidden, Joseph would tell another good man whom he loved very dearly, called Alan, to go to a certain stream and catch a silver fish that he would see swimming about in the clear water. Alan would go willingly; and, however often he went, he always saw the silver fish gleaming and flashing among the singing bubbles of the stream. He would catch the fish and bring it to the bright table to show to Joseph, who would then tell him to take it and broil it on a fire of clear embers. When this was done, Alan served the fish to the people who sat about the silver table. However many there were to feed, the fish always went around, and when the feast was over, everybody who had shared in it felt happy, content, and joyful, strong to do what was right and to resist what was wrong. They would go away glad and grateful, wondering how it was that Alan could always catch so magical and marvelous a fish. They never really understood the secret, which belonged to him and to Joseph alone, but they gave him the name of the Rich Fisher, and as the Rich Fisher he has been known for many hundreds of years.

Well, month after month, the silver table was spread, the Grail Cup was displayed, and the mysterious fish was served by the Rich Fisher. But wicked men ruled the country in which Joseph lived, and they had already once thrown him into prison because he would not give up his Cup. They were again plotting against him when, one day as he worked in his garden, he was visited by

The Shining Cup

a beautiful spirit, who told him that he must take the Grail to a distant country, called West-over-the-Sea. Joseph asked how this could be done, "For," said he, "I am only a gardener and a worker in the cornfields, and I have no ship in which to voyage, nor sailor-friends to manage its oars and sails." The bright spirit, however, bade him have faith and not be afraid. He was just to set off with his children and his friends, and they were to carry the silver table and the Shining Cup with them. Then the vision faded away among the vines and dark cedar trees, and Joseph went into his house, and, sending for the Rich Fisher, told him, and everybody else, to make ready for the journey.

Well, they set off as soon as they could: Joseph, the Rich Fisher, their children, and their friends. They carried the silver table carefully, and Joseph bore the Shining Cup in a casket set with hundreds of precious stones. After traveling for many days, they reached the seashore; there lay the deep blue ocean ahead of them, rosy-purple in the far distance, and overhung with the clouds of sunset, all delicate and golden, looking like enchanted islands. One of these, everybody felt quite sure, must be the home chosen for the Grail Cup —the honored island called West-over-the-Sea.

But between them and the enchanted islands of the sunset, the sea moved its long, murmuring, empty waves. Not a ship's sail was to be seen; not a single little boat rocked in the green furrows near the shore. Joseph stood at the edge of the water, perplexed and wondering; and the sunset light fell on his white under-robe and scarlet mantle. As he stood, with everybody watching him, a voice suddenly floated across the shore.

"Take off your white under-robe, Joseph, and spread it upon the sea."

Joseph heard the voice, and while his people gazed in wonder, he took off his white under-robe, and, stepping into the ripples, spread the soft hand-sewn linen out upon the water. It floated like a beautiful raft; and Joseph heard the voice a second time, falling as musically as the song of a bird through the quiet evening air:

"Step forward and take your stand upon it, and let all your people follow you."

Joseph moved forward and, lifting high the casket which held the Grail Cup, stepped upon this strange white boat. The linen garment was firm to his feet, and rocked up and down like a strong ship at anchor. He stood there, fearless and upright, and called to all his people to join him. In twos and threes they came, amazed but trustful, bringing with them the silver table, while Joseph still held up the casket in which the Shining Cup was safely hidden. Room was found for everyone upon the floating white robe, and the silver table was set in the very middle of them all. Then, as soon as they had gathered around Jo-

The Shining Cup

seph, some strange power stirred the quiet ripples of the sea, the linen robe began to move from the shore, and in a very few minutes, the Keeper of the Grail Cup, with Alan the Rich Fisher, and all their children and grandchildren, found themselves traveling swiftly and smoothly across the ocean in the direction of West-over-the-Sea.

The sun sank, the moon rose, and still the white linen robe, with all these people clustered together upon it, sailed, faster than any ship, over the starlit water. Then, by and by, the moon set, too, and the sun came up again into the sky behind the travelers. As it rose, it threw its beams, all golden, upon the fresh, wakening world; and Joseph cried out, joyfully, that he could see the sandy beaches, the high cliffs, and the distant mountains of West-over-the-Sea.

Surely enough, there lay the land, sparkling and beautiful. But as the travelers drew nearer, they saw that, while they had left warmth and flowers and fruiting trees behind them, they had come to a country where winter reigned. All was cold and snow-covered. The rocks glittered with the frosts of the night; the streams were hushed under the silence of the ice. The outspread robe floated into a little bay, and the chill winds of the north blew upon the voyagers' faces as, one by one, they stepped down into the icy ripples and hurried breathlessly to the shore.

Joseph came last of all, and as he left his strange ship, the voice came again, down from the mountains, telling him to lift his robe and put it once more upon his shoulders. He did so, and behold! it was quite warm and dry. Then he and the Rich Fisher led all the people up a narrow pathway which climbed the cliffside. And still Joseph bore the Grail, while some of the others willingly carried the silver table between them.

They reached the top of the cliff, and then they traveled onward, over mountains and through valleys, until they reached a place called Glastonbury. And Joseph knew that here he was meant to build a little church of wood. He leaned on his staff for a long time, looking round with joy in his eyes. It seemed to him a wonderful thing that he was to build a church in the island of Britain, which was the real name of West-over-the-Sea.

Then, as he leaned on his staff, he felt it move and tremble strangely under his hand. He glanced down, and lo! he saw little twigs and stems sprouting out on all sides of it, laden with green leaves and pale whitethorn flowers. Taking his hand from it, startled, he perceived that it had rooted in the frost-bound earth! He touched the tiny flowers wonderingly; and even as he touched them, snow began to fall and mingle its feathery flakes with the pearly petals. Then the staff shot upward, and great boughs, all covered

The Shining Cup

with blossom, branched about Joseph's figure and high above his head. In a few minutes, he was standing, amazed, under a spreading thorn tree, laden with sweet-smelling snow-white bloom!

Then Joseph called the Rich Fisher to him. He called, too, to all his followers—who stood as amazed as himself—and told them to set down the silver table under the flowering tree. They did so, and the Rich Fisher, in obedience to Joseph, went to a little half-frozen stream close at hand. There, swimming about close to the edge of the ice, he saw the beautiful gleaming fish. He caught it quickly and, making a fire of sticks, roasted it upon the clear embers. Then, coming back to the silver table, he saw that Joseph had set the Shining Cup in the midst of it, and that everybody was prepared to share in the magical feast. So there, under the blossoming thorn tree, the children and followers of Joseph and the Rich Fisher ate their first banquet at West-over-the-Sea, while the snow fell thickly all about them and covered the fields and plain of Glastonbury with a mantle of whiteness.

Now, while they were feasting, an old man dressed in a long robe, who was called a Druid, passed by, and paused, utterly amazed at what he saw. Well might he be surprised to see these Eastern people, in their blue and purple and scarlet robes, seated round a silver table under a tree all covered with flowers. He looked at them in wonder, and, in greater wonder, gazed at a beautiful Cup which was set in the middle of the table, which shone as delicately as a little moonlit cloud. Even while he watched, the banquet came to an end. The strangers stood up; the one who seemed to be chief took the Cup into his hands; others lifted the silver table; and, unaware that they were seen by the old Druid, they all swept away in a radiant procession toward the inland forests, leaving the blossoming tree standing, mysterious and beautiful, under the falling snow.

The Druid stepped up to the tree, touched it, and smelled the flowers. Then he went back to the grove of oaks in which he lived and wrote down all that he had seen in a parchment book with gold clasps to it. This book he locked up, and it was kept hidden for many years; but Merlin heard of it, and one day, long, long afterwards, he came to Glastonbury, found it, and read it. What he did after he had read the book you will be told in another story. But meanwhile, Joseph, and the Rich Fisher, and their friends sought the King of the country, and he gave them the piece of land where the thorn tree was blossoming for their own. So they built a little wooden church there, and the country people worshiped in it for many years.

King Mordrain's Perilous Island

At the time the Grail Cup was carried to Britain, many strange things took place all over the world. One of the strangest was an adventure which happened to a heathen King called Mordrain, who had known Joseph, and had become a Christian on account of the things that Joseph had taught him. Mordrain was out hunting one day when his horses took fright at the thunder and lightning of a great storm. They galloped off with the chariot in which the King sat; and he would probably have been killed had not a mysterious hand and arm, like the hand and arm of a giant, come out of one of the blackest clouds, lifted him bodily, swung him through the storm-riven air, and set him down on an island in the middle of the ocean!

There, then, was King Mordrain, wet, cold, and entirely desolate. The island was nothing but a great pile of rugged rocks, with caves running deeply within them. Once it had been the home of brigands; but now not even a brigand was left to keep poor King Mordrain company. He was terribly hungry; and, as he climbed about the rocks, he thought he would certainly die of famine and thirst. But when he had given up the hope of finding fruit to eat, or fresh water to drink, in this dreary waste, he caught sight, all at once, of the prettiest little ship in the world, fluttering like a butterfly out of the blackness of the storm. Mast, sails, and rigging were all lily-white, and shone beneath the dark clouds. A red cross, like the cross that you may see nowadays on the banner of St. George of England, floated just above the bow; and under the crimson cross, a man with a kind, beautiful face stood erect, gazing toward the perilous rocks of the desolate island.

This pretty red-and-white ship came sailing on, and, slipping between the jagged rocks, paused at last almost at the feet of the astonished King. As it lay, moving softly up and down in its sheltered nook, the man struck a harp which he held, and began to sing. While he sang, it seemed as if a delicious fragrance floated from the ship, so that Mordrain felt as if he stood in a valley of wild flowers. He shut his eyes, and he thought that sweet cool grass was springing up about his feet and the hem of his sea-wetted robe. He thought, too, that trees with rosy apples on them grew within reach of his hand; that corn, all ripe and yellow, waved beyond the trees; and that, farther still, sleek gentle cows were walking homeward to be milked. Still the man in the bows of the ship sang on; and then Mordrain thought that he was drinking the cows' sweet milk, biting joyfully

into the red apples, and eating white, delicate bread made from the ground wheat. All the time, the song continued, and the King caught the echo of the words.

"I am the minstrel who sails the seas from port to port. I make beautiful the things which once were ugly and vile. I give riches to the poor, health to the sick, happiness to the sorrowful! To you, O sad and weary King, I give the refreshing food and drink of which you are in such great need!"

The song ceased, and Mordrain opened his eyes. There were no flowers, no apples, no delicious bread made from ripe wheat. Nothing was to be seen but the salt ocean, the cruel rocks, and the little white ship with the man who sang in the bows under a red cross like the cross on the banner of St. George. But Mordrain felt as if he had just risen from the most delicious feast in the world! His eyes were bright, his cheeks had lost their paleness, and he stood upright, strong and happy. But, just as he was going to beg the minstrel to land, the whole ship vanished from sight! It seemed either to have been swallowed by the waves or caught up into the sky. Instead of the delicate white sails, the glowing red cross, Mordrain saw another ship driving fast through the water, out of the north. This vessel was richly fitted and inlaid with thousands of jewels. Its sails were like black velvet; and under their mysteri-

King Mordrain's Perilous Island

ous shadow sat the most beautiful woman the King had ever seen in his life.

This woman, too, was singing as the ship drove into the little creek among the rocks. But Mordrain, listening, knew, somehow, that her song was evil. She sang of a palace where she reigned as Queen, to which she wanted to carry the King in her boat with the black velvet sails. She promised him wealth, and ease, and luxury such as he had never known. All the time she sang, the lightning flashed upon the jewels on the mast and rigging; the thunder pealed solemnly about the rocks, and rolled and muttered round the cliff above. Over and over again, Mordrain was on the point of stepping onto the boat and telling the beautiful wicked woman that he would sail away with her to her own land. But something always held him back.

At last, as a vivid lightning flash wrapped all the ship in blue flame, while the thunder crashed like cannon, the song suddenly ceased. When Mordrain's eyes were cleared from the blindness which had fallen upon them for a moment's space, both ship and singer had vanished in the storm.

Great waves were breaking over the rocks now, and the King climbed higher up the cliff and took shelter in a deep cave. All night he heard the seas and winds roaring, but toward morning, both sky and water became calm. Mordrain fell asleep, and dreamed that, once more, he stood in the valley of flowers. Waking up, he smelled their fragrance; and, peeping out of his cave, he saw, again, the pretty ship rocking in the harbor, with its lily-white sails, its red cross, and its minstrel making music on his harp in the clear, still morning air.

How glad Mordrain was to see the minstrel again! He hurried down the rocks to meet him, and told him of the beautiful evil woman on the ship with the black sails. The minstrel listened gravely; and when the King had finished his story, he told him that the woman was really a demon in disguise, who would have flung him into the sea and left him to perish.

"And, King Mordrain," said the minstrel, "you are one of those who have been chosen to follow the Grail-People into West-over-the-Sea, and to find the hiding place in which the Shining Cup has been safely placed by Joseph. But you must never follow any leader, nor sail from this island in any ship, unless you see the cross that one day will shine red upon the white banner of England. That banner, only, is the true banner for you—that sign, only, the true sign which will lead you to the hiding place of the Cup that people know now as the *Holy* Grail."

The minstrel and the ship vanished once more, but Mordrain was left refreshed and comforted.

Another day passed, night came, and the King slept calmly in his cave. He went out just as the morning star was fading, and, behold! a third ship was sailing toward the island over the dawn-lit sea.

Mordrain gazed, and gazed, and suddenly his face grew radiant with delight. He recognized the ship—it had lain always at anchor in his own royal bay! He saw the sails, and knew their rig! Familiar forms of his own courtiers crowded in the bows—familiar faces were turned upon him, familiar voices called and shouted his name! His children were there—his palace servants—his very war-horse stamped and neighed on deck, held by his own pretty page. King Mordrain waved his hands, his arms, shouted back to the courtiers, cried out the name of the horse. Only for one moment did he pause before leaping down the rocks to meet his friends—only for one moment, to look, and look in vain, for the banner with the red cross upon it, which was to be the banner under which he had been told to serve.

"It is not there! But what can it matter? This is my own royal vessel; these are my own courtiers and children and servants! No demons can be aboard *this* ship to do me harm!"

The King thrust away the thought of the red cross, and, still calling his glad greetings, sprang onto the deck of the ship. Suddenly he paused—a feeling of terror had seized him the moment that his foot touched the boards. The courtiers pressed to greet him, but he waved them back.

He thought he saw a vision of the banner floating at the helm; and, putting up his fingers, he passed them over the faint, dim image of the red cross. Instantly a clap of thunder sounded, and everybody on the ship vanished—courtiers, children, servants, horse and page! King Mordrain was left on the skeleton of a ship without pilot, sailors, sails, or rigging. And this skeleton of a ship began slowly moving out of the harbor into the great empty sea.

King Mordrain called aloud, then. He turned to the east, the west, the north, the south, calling upon the beautiful minstrel to save him. No white boat appeared; but on the horizon, the King saw a slow, dim sweeping of wings. Then, out of the blue distance, came two birds like shining eagles, and they carried a knight, with a wonderful, pitiful face, between them. They paused near Mordrain's terrible ship, and began slowly floating round and round. As they did so, the knight with the brave, gentle face stooped toward the water and seemed to trace something upon the waves. Mordrain, watching the movement of his hand, thought that, under the white foam of the sea, he saw, again, the red cross that he had been told would shine one day on the white banner of St. George.

Then the knight called to the King, and bade him take the rudder, and follow the flight of the birds, for he was Mordrain's appointed guardian, and would lead him to safety. And the two great birds turned westward, and Mordrain followed them, carried mysteriously in the ship without sailors and without sails, until he reached West-over-the-Sea, and landed on the shore on the very spot where Joseph and the Rich Fisher had landed with the silver table and the Shining Cup of the Holy Grail.

The Fiery Star

One dark and stormy night Merlin stood at one of his seventy windows, and kept looking, and looking, and looking up at the wild sky. He was expecting to see something there: something very unusual and wonderful, which one of his fairy books had told him to expect. For a long time, however, nothing happened. The watching magician only saw the clouds racing like inky shadows over the clear high spaces that were sprinkled with stars. Then, all at once, he caught sight of a little pearly glimmer in the north. This little pearly glimmer grew brighter and brighter; it turned from silver to gold, and from gold to a deep, shining red, like the red of rubies. Merlin gazed still more eagerly, and presently, in the heart of the red glow, he saw a great star brighten, as you might see a crimson fire suddenly break into a shining flame. From the great star one ray shot out suddenly, brilliant as a diamond and slender as a knight's spear. At the end of the ray appeared a globe of fire, which, as Merlin still watched, uncoiled itself slowly and took the shape of a beautiful and terrible dragon. This fiery dragon opened its mouth and sent out two more rays, one to the east, the other to the west. The eastern ray seemed to have no end to it, but disappeared in brightness, so that you might almost have thought the sun was just going to rise. The ray to the west went into the night shadows and then broke up into seven smaller rays, which spread themselves in a golden fan above the shadowy peaks of the distant hills.

When Merlin had seen all this happen, he laughed gladly, and, flying down the long staircase of his fairy home as lightly as a bird or a butterfly, he set off on invisible wings through the night. Always the fiery dragon shone in the sky overhead; and Merlin knew that its bright form was hanging just over the castle of Uther, the King. As the wizard drew near to the castle, he dropped onto his feet on the grass and took on the form of an old man, wrapped in a cloak. With his white beard blowing about him in the wind, and the hood of the cloak drawn down over his eyes and forehead, Merlin walked up to the castle gates and knocked loudly with his staff.

Now, all this time the great flaming dragon was lying, stretched out in the sky, steeping the towers and turrets of the castle in a crimson light, fiery and terrible. The guards and servants, the porters, the cooks, and the pages had seen it, and were frightened out of their wits. Nobody dared to answer the door at first, so Merlin knocked

The Fiery Star

again, much more loudly. Then, when a terrified porter appeared, the magician, in a voice of authority, demanded to be taken to the presence of the King.

There was something in Merlin's voice that the porter dared not disobey. He hurriedly opened the great gate and let the old man in. Then he led Merlin through the courtyard—all lit up by the dragon—down the great stone corridor, across the hall, hung with gorgeous tapestry, where terrified pages waited, dressed in satins and silks. Then the porter paused and pointed; and Merlin went on alone right into the royal apartment of the King.

King Uther sat on his throne, pale and grave, and quite alone. Through a great window, curtainless and arched, came the fiery glow from the dragon in the sky. It stained the fresh green rushes on the floor with crimson, and shone all about the solitary figure of the King. Uther looked up at the sound of footsteps, and saw an old man coming slowly up the room, wrapped in a long cloak, with a snow-white beard that streamed, in long, thick strands, far below his waist.

"Who are you? Why do you come here unbidden and unannounced?" demanded the King sternly. But before he finished speaking, the old man threw back his cloak and Uther saw who he was.

"Merlin—my friend Merlin!" he cried in an

altered voice. "I am indeed glad you have come! What means this blazing and terrible dragon in the sky? Is it a sign of some cruel disaster, some great trouble, that is about to fall upon my house?"

Then Merlin answered. His voice sounded so glad and triumphant that King Uther knew the news was good even before the magician gave it.

"The dragon is the most wonderful sign that has ever shone in the sky above the castle of a King," cried Merlin. "I have been watching for it night after night, hoping and longing to see it come! It means that to you, and to the beautiful lady you love, a little Prince will be born. This little Prince will be the greatest King the world ever saw. He will reign over many subjects, and will conquer all his enemies. He is the ray from the mouth of the dragon that goes to the east, and he will be as bright and beautiful as the rising sun. The ray that goes to the west, and breaks up into seven rays, is your daughter. She will be, not only a Princess, but a fairy, and have seven fairy children, who will teach the men-children of the West the songs that fairies sing. See how the seven rays end in a shining mist! That is the meaning of the fiery dragon, King Uther—the meaning that I have hurried into your presence to explain!"

Uther listened breathlessly, and, all the time, the light from the dragon shone crimson upon the faces and hands and robes of the old wizard and the young King. Then Uther leaned forward and pressed his fingers on Merlin's arm.

"My beautiful lady?" he said eagerly. "Do you mean Ygierne?"

He could hardly wait for Merlin's reply, because he had loved Ygierne for months, but she was shut up in a castle, quite out of his reach.

"Yes, I mean Ygierne," answered Merlin. "I promise that you shall have her for your bride. I promise, too, that you and she shall have this bright and beautiful Prince and this fairylike Princess for your children. But if you are to marry Ygierne through my help, you must make me a promise in return."

"What is that?" asked Uther. "Tell me! There is no promise that I would not make for the sake of beautiful Ygierne!"

"You must promise that as soon as your little son is born, you will give him into my care. He has a great work to do in the world, and can only learn to do it if I have the charge of him. Give me *your* promise, Uther, and I will set about the performance of *mine!*"

King Uther, for a moment, felt uncertain and sad. Where would be the gladness in a little princely son if the child was to be taken away from him as soon as he was born? But he loved Ygierne so passionately that, after hesitating for one second more, he consented.

"Very well, Merlin!" he cried. "Very well! You shall have my little son to bring up as your own child, if you will only make it possible for me to marry my beautiful lady, Ygierne!"

The red shining through the window, which fell from the fiery dragon in the sky, grew stronger and fiercer as Uther spoke. When he had given the promise the light blazed crimson and terrible about the throne on which he sat, and showed up all the diamonds and sapphires in his scepter and crown. A peal of thunder rolled above the palace; a flash of lightning darted about the gray stone towers. The blazing dragon seemed to close its jaws. As it closed them, the rays drew slowly back into its great mouth—the one ray from the east and the seven rays from the west. It stretched out its long, fiery claws, and two great golden wings rose, waving, over its great golden head. Then, all at once, it spread out these wings and hung, poised, above the castle, so that all the pages and cooks and scullions and porters hid themselves in the darkest corners and cupboards and cellars they could find! But instead of swooping down upon the castle, as they expected, the blazing dragon struck its wings together once —twice—thrice. Once, twice, thrice, the thunder pealed out again; and before its echoes had died away, the fiery creature had shot, swift as an arrow, far through the night sky, leaving a long tail of starry light, like the tail of a comet, behind it.

The Fiery Star

Even King Uther had crouched for a moment and covered his face. When he took his jeweled satin cloak from his eyes, the royal throne room was empty, dark, and still. Merlin had vanished with the dragon, and had gone back to the fairy house of seventy windows and sixty doors. The King was left alone, with the promise of a beautiful bride and a wonderful little son.

The King stepped down from his throne and went to the window. He looked up to the sky, and saw it dark and clear, silvered over with quiet little stars. Then he summoned a herald (who came, trembling still) and told him to take his trumpet and go through the castle, crying aloud these words:

"King Uther has been told the meaning of the blazing dragon in the sky. It is a sign of great gladness, and victory, and well-being for himself and for his kingdom. From now, the King will be known as King Uther Pendragon, and he lays commands on his royal sculptors that two golden dragons immediately be made. One of these dragons will be set up in the capital of his kingdom. The other will be carried by his royal standard-bearer into every battle. These are the orders of Uther Pendragon, King of the lordly and ancient country of Britain!"

The Round Table of Oak

Merlin, the great wizard, was the best friend of Uther, the good King. The stories told about the magician's fairy house in the woods were quite true; and Merlin spent most of his time in his wonderful home among the pine trees, looking from one or the other of the seventy windows, or passing in and out of one or the other of the sixty doors. What a strange, shadowy place it was, to be sure, with wild deer feeding in the glades that surrounded it and wild geese clanging as they flew in flocks across the sky at night. Human beings never ventured very far into this mysterious wood, but they whispered all sorts of tales about it to each other as they sat over their big log fires in the evenings. They named it the Enchanted Forest; or, sometimes, the Valley of No Return. Hunters who followed the hares over the meadows, or chased the wild boars through the tangled thickets on the edge of the woodland, always stopped short, and turned their horses and their hounds about, when they looked into the dark shadows of these haunted trees. Sometimes they caught glimpses of gray walls and towers, and heard sounds like fairies singing, or unseen horses trampling, or invisible hounds baying through the wood. Then the real horses and hounds would begin to tremble as the hunters hurried them away. But nobody could ever quite describe what he had seen and heard: though all were agreed that if any rash person ventured up to the dim, gray walls of Merlin's home, he was pretty certain never to come back.

In this hidden house, then, Merlin learned all sorts of things from the fairies, because he could see and hear and speak to the invisible people of the air. He learned so many of their secrets that at last he became a regular fairy-king among them. Not only would the wild stags carry him wherever he wanted to go, but all the good fairy-folk would come up out of the streams and down from the stars whenever he called them. As for the wicked fairy-men, he left them alone on the top of their mountain. They might be his uncles, and his cousins, and his grandfathers, and his great-grandfathers, but he had much nicer friends among the kindly fairies, to say nothing of the human kings and princes, and suchlike comfortable earthly folk of royal or noble blood.

One day Merlin was standing under a great oak tree, just after the sun had set and the quiet shadows had commenced to steal through his beautiful wood. The little birds had stopped singing, and the bats were beginning to flit about. Merlin

The Round Table of Oak

felt that something rather wonderful was going to happen—something beautiful and strange, by which even the fairy-folk of the Enchanted Forest would be greatly amazed. The evening grew darker, and, all at once, the oak boughs above his head began to rustle and whisper, as if a little wind were moving them up and down. At the same time, he heard soft knockings inside the tree trunk, and a murmur of many voices speaking together in what seemed to be an unknown foreign tongue.

Then, in the middle of the shadows, the branches and trunk of the oak began to give out a silver shining, like the shining of a full moon. Slowly and silently, a great clearness grew round about the tree. The boughs seemed to fade away, and a wonderful picture appeared, painted on the bright air—the picture of an old man with a long white beard, standing before a silver table on which was a mysterious and beautiful Shining Cup. About the table many people were seated; they wore gay Eastern robes, and looked very calm and content. And by the side of the old man with the white beard stood a younger man, with a silver fish in his hands. He placed the fish on the table, and everyone stood up. Merlin thought he heard them singing as they did so, but the sound seemed to come from very far away. Then the whole bright vision faded; the silver table, and the Shining Cup, and the gaily dressed people disappeared; and Merlin found himself alone in the forest again, with the oak leaves whispering and rustling above his head.

But while he stood wondering, behold! a little book suddenly fell down from the branches to his feet. As it fell, he heard a voice speaking among the leaves:

"In the little book is written the story of the silver table and the Shining Cup that you have been allowed to see in a vision! I, who speak to you, am the old Druid who saw them brought to the land of West-over-the-Sea. I have been commanded to show you the vision, and to give you the little book. Also, I have been commanded to tell you that from the wood of the oak tree, in whose boughs you have seen the vision, you are to carve another Round Table, like the Silver Table on which the Shining Cup stood. When you have carved this second Round Table, you are to take it to King Uther and bid him keep it carefully in his palace until his death. For it will have a marvelous meaning and purpose for many years to come."

The voice died away, and even Merlin, magician though he was, could not see the spirit of the old Druid, which had visited him in the Enchanted Forest and brought the mysterious old book. But he picked up the book and took it home to his fairy house. There he lit his lamp and, sitting down among his magic volumes and crystals and strange caskets and boxes, read the book from end to end. And in it was the whole story of Joseph and his followers, and the church made of wood at Glastonbury, and the beautiful Christmas-flowering thorn. Not only was the whole tale written down in the book, but there were also careful directions about the making of the second Round Table, which was to be carved from the oak in whose branches Merlin had seen the vision, and, when finished, given into the care of Uther, the King.

Merlin locked the book up carefully in one of his caskets, for he knew what a very, very precious possession it was. Many years after, the little book fell into the hands of another good old man, who was very like the long-dead Glastonbury Druid himself. It came to him just as it came to Merlin, falling from the boughs of a tree that was lit up with mysterious light, while a voice spoke softly among the rustling leaves. And—so people would have told you in those days—it was through the writing in the little old book that they knew all about the silver table, and the Rich Fisher, and the hidden secrets of the Holy Grail.

Meanwhile, however, Merlin kept the little book locked up, and set to work to make a big Round Table from the oak tree in the wood. Nobody knows exactly how he made it, but the fairyfolk helped him, and he found words written in the little book that were obeyed by invisible hands using invisible axes and saws and hammers and nails. When he had finished he was even a greater magician than he had been when he had begun—so great that, by using certain spells, he was able to lift the Round Table straight out of his house in the Enchanted Forest, and to set it down in the very middle of the royal castle that belonged to Uther, the King.

Well, Uther was greatly amazed when he saw this beautiful and big Round Table, brought to his castle nobody knew how. As he gazed at it, however, he became aware that Merlin was standing by him, smiling at his astonishment. The magician told him something, though not all, of the way in which the table had been made, and Uther looked at him admiringly.

"You seem to me to be able to do anything you wish to, Merlin!" he exclaimed. "I wish you would bring me the Giants' Dance from Ireland!"

"What is the Giants' Dance?" asked Merlin. He knew quite well, really, but he was pretending that he did not.

King Uther told him, then, that he had just come back from a war in Ireland, and that, among the hills, there was an extraordinary circle of great stones, which the people said were enchanted giants, and which they always called the Giants' Dance. He had wished very much to bring this circle home with him, and had set a whole army to work to try and lift the stones from their places and set them on the ships that were waiting to carry them away. But, though all the engineers of those days had worked their hardest and done their best, none of them could lift the great stones so much as an inch out of the ground. In despair, Uther had given up the idea of bringing the stones to his own kingdom, and had left them standing, in their wide, still, lonely magnificence, on the distant Irish hills.

"Oh!" said Merlin. "It's just a great circle of stones you want moving, is it? Well, that's easily done!"

Off he set for Ireland, with his crystal balls, and his black wands, and his lists of spells that were written down in his fairy books. But the small old book of the Holy Grail he left at home. When he reached the hill where the Giants' Dance stood, he went up to the top quite alone. What he said and did there nobody ever knew! But the peasants who lived in huts in the valley told a strange story of what some of them had seen that night— a story about great stones that traveled, all alone and upright, down the slopes of the mountain, while voices, which guided their movements, called down from the air and up from the ground! They told, too, of great ships with shadowy sails that were seen setting out to sea. And the movements of the ships were guided by voices calling among the waves. However this might have been, whether the peasants really saw these things or only dreamed them, certain it is that the next morning the Giants' Dance had been carried away from Ireland and set up, not very far from Uther's castle, on Salisbury Plain!

And on Salisbury Plain it stands to this day, but we call it Stonehenge now, and have almost forgotten that it was once called the Giants' Dance. While as for the Round Table, you may see a Round Table for yourselves at Winchester: though that is only a copy of the table that Merlin made in his fairy palace in the middle of the Valley of No Return.

The Sword
in the Great White Stone

Ygierne, as you know, was shut up in a castle where Uther could never visit her, though he had admired and loved her from a distance for a very long time. But Merlin kept his promise, and, by his magic, made Uther able to take on the face and figure and voice of the lord of the castle, so that the King could come and go without anyone finding out. Merlin was always rather inclined to think that "all is fair in love and war"; and, as he knew the future, he knew that Uther was destined to marry the lady Ygierne in the end. So he did not scruple to help matters forward a little; and when the lord of the castle was killed in battle, Ygierne knew nothing about it, but thought he was having supper with her, quite comfortably, as usual. Of course her visitor was really Uther Pendragon, who came to her in his own form a little later. Then he told her that he loved her, and would always protect her, though the castle in which she had lived so long had fallen into other hands. So she married him and became his Queen; and long, long afterwards, he confessed to her that he used to visit her in her old home in disguise, because he loved her so deeply and truly that he could not bear to be away from her for many days at a time.

After the marriage, King Uther Pendragon and his sweet and lovely lady Ygierne lived very happily in a castle called Tintagel, by the Cornish Sea. You may see the ruins of it now, but you can never perhaps imagine how fine and strong it was in those days, hundreds of years ago. Great gray towers towered above great gray roofs; and archers practiced shooting from the strong high walls. Sometimes the big gates and doors were closed—sometimes they opened wide to let out large companies of soldiers, dressed in bright armor and riding on handsome, spirited horses, with gay bridles and reins. In the evenings, sounds of music and laughter came from inside. Minstrels with harps played and sang to the King and Queen; and funny dwarfs, in caps and bells, made jokes, or danced absurd little dances among the rushes on the floor. Oh, it was a wonderful place, was Tintagel, and you will never see anything like it nowadays! Folks were brave and cheerful then, and though they certainly had terrible battles with their neighbors, they were so gay and courageous between-times that their lives passed as happily as possible, between work and play, banquets and tournaments. The knights loved and fought for the fair ladies. The fair ladies loved and looked after the knights. And bravest, most

The Sword in the Great White Stone 63

loving, and fairest of all were King Uther Pendragon and Ygierne, the Queen.

Well, they were very happy together at Tintagel, and by and by, their little son was born. Ygierne knew, now, that Uther had promised to give the baby instantly into Merlin's charge. She was very sad about this, but she would not ask the King to break his word. Besides, she and Uther had often talked of the great future which Merlin had foretold for their child. So the King and Queen kissed the baby Prince, and the Queen herself wrapped him up in a beautiful cloak of cloth-of-gold and gave him into the charge of two ladies and two knights. Then Uther told the two ladies and the two knights to carry the tiny Prince to a certain little half-hidden door in the castle wall, to open this door softly and silently, and to give the child into the arms of somebody who would be waiting just outside to receive it.

Singing soft little lullabies, the two ladies stepped carefully down the corridor, followed by the two knights. They reached the winding stairs and went down, down, down to the little half-hidden door. One lady carried the baby on a golden cushion, asleep in its golden cloak. The other carried a tall candle; and the two knights, walking behind, carried two more candles, taller still.

They opened the door, and the light of the candles shone out into the dark, still night. From among the shadows came a dim, tall figure, not unlike a shadow itself. This figure held out its hands for the baby, and the ladies and the knights gave the tiny boy into the stranger's arms. Then they went back through the door with their candles, and the empty golden cushion; and, as they climbed up, up, up the winding staircase, they heard the distant, dying trotting of a horse.

On the horse rode Merlin with the baby. Over hill and dale he went until he reached a quiet small castle in a valley. Here lived a good and sober knight called Sir Hector, who knew well why Merlin had come. Long ago, the magician and King Uther had sent for Sir Hector and asked him if he would receive a little child into his house—a little child who was to become very great and famous, but who must be brought up simply as a noble knight's son. He had consented, and had been given lands and riches in return. So when Merlin rode up in the dark night, Sir Hector and his wife met the magician gladly and took the baby straight to their own nursery. Then Merlin had the little Prince christened "Arthur"; and Sir Hector brought him up in his own good, quiet, and happy home.

But Merlin was always at hand, watching over the boy. His father, King Uther, was content to leave little Arthur in the great wizard's charge. However, when he was dying, he sent for Merlin and asked for news of the child.

How happy he was when he heard that Prince

The Sword in the Great White Stone

Arthur was growing up into a beautiful little boy, already asking to ride his horse, hunt his hounds, and shoot his arrows with the others. How much better it was that he should, later, be brought up just as a good knight, instead of as a king's favored son! Uther listened gladly, certain now that his sacrifice of his baby had not been made in vain. Then he gave the Round Table back to Merlin, and told him how it might be kept safe and sound until Arthur came into his kingdom. Accordingly, Merlin had it carried far away to Cameliard, where it was placed in the care of an old friend of Uther's, another great King, whose name was Leodogran, who, in his turn, put it into the charge of two hundred and fifty knights, all of them brave, noble, and good. What happened to it afterwards you will hear in another story.

So Uther died, but nobody knew that the little lad in Sir Hector's house was the dead King's son and heir. The barons of the country began to quarrel, tooth and nail, among themselves. Each of them wanted the power to rule over the rest. Never was there such an uncomfortable commotion! Wherever you went, you would meet soldiers on horseback, shaking their spears and shouting out fine speeches about their own baron, and angry speeches about the barons of other people. The woods and meadows rang with the sound of steel and the thunder of horses' hoofs. So that at last Merlin went to the Archbishop, who mourned over these things very sorrowfully in his lonely palace of peace, and told him to call all the warring barons to London for Christmas, that they might go to service in the church and forget their quarrels, if it were only for the short and gentle hours of Christmas Day.

The barons dared not disobey the Archbishop, so to London and to church they duly went. The service over, out streamed the congregation into the churchyard. And there they saw something that had assuredly not been visible when they went in.

Right in the east of the churchyard, lit by the pale Christmas sun, stood a stone white as marble, but a thousand times more beautiful. In the center of it was a square of steel, and from the steel rose the glittering handle of a strong, sharp sword. In letters of gold about the sword were written strange and thrilling words—words which said that whoever could draw the sword out of the stone was King of Britain, Uther Pendragon's only rightful heir.

The barons crowded round the stone, wide-eyed and amazed. Each called out that he, if given a chance, was certainly the one and only chieftain who could draw the sword from the stone. Smiling oddly, Merlin, who stood near, bade them all try. Jostling each other in their hurry, they sprang, one by one, to the side of the stone, seized the handle of the sword, and pulled and tugged

The Sword in the Great White Stone 67

with all their might. But their efforts were not a bit of good. The sword did not even tremble in its square of steel, while the golden letters written around it seemed to mock the barons with their quiet, sure message for the chieftain who was the unknown rightful King.

At last, the barons, tired and angry, went away from the churchyard and began to amuse themselves by holding a tournament in some meadows not very far away. After all, it was Christmastime—the season for junketings, jaunts, and knightly games. And riding to the tournament as a matter of course came Sir Hector, his son Sir Kay, and the fair and noble boy Arthur, whom Sir Hector loved as much as his own child.

As they passed the churchyard, they saw the sword, shining always in the stone that was like beautiful white marble, and they spoke to each other of the strangeness of the sight. Then they trotted forward, each on a handsome horse. But just as they were about to ride into the meadow, so bright with banners and gay with voices, Sir Kay exclaimed, in utter dismay, that he could take no share in the delights of the tournament, for he had left his own sword at home!

"Turn your horse quickly, my son," said Sir Hector to young Arthur. "Gallop home and fetch your brother's sword. *You* are too young for the knightly games, but *he* must on no account be left out of them."

Arthur did not wait to be told a second time. Home he went, full speed, to fetch his elder "brother's" sword. But when he reached the house, everything was lonely and locked up. Sir Hector's lady had gone to the tournament herself, and had taken all the servants with her!

For a minute or two, Arthur hesitated. Then he was struck by the very happiest thought. "I will go to the churchyard," said he, "and will take the sword that is sticking out of the big white stone! It will do just as well for my brother as his own!"

So he mounted his horse again and off to the churchyard he rode. Dismounting, he hastened to the great stone. There, not even pausing to read the words which were written in the golden letters, he took the sword by the handle and pulled. Lo and behold! the sword came as easily and lightly from the steel in the middle of the marble as a rose might come from the delicate green shelter of its bush.

Sword in hand, Arthur once more sprang into the saddle and galloped away to the tournament. Over the meadow grass he trotted, and straight into the hands of Sir Kay he gave the sword. Then, like the lighthearted, modest boy he was, he fell back among the other younglings, watching to see his elder brother's triumph with an eager and delighted expectancy.

But Sir Kay was staring with all his eyes at the

sword. He turned it this way and that, then rode off to where his father, also, watched him from a distance.

"Sir," he said to Sir Hector, "this sword which young Arthur has brought me is the very sword that no baron could draw from the stone in the east of the churchyard! You have heard what was written around it in letters of gold?"

"I have heard," said Sir Hector, grave and startled. For he, too, had been told the story of the sword set so firmly in the beautiful white stone! He, too, recognized it as it glittered in his son's hand.

"If this is so, sir," cried Sir Kay, with a glowing face, "then I—*I*—must be King of Britain, Uther Pendragon's heir!"

But Sir Hector, deep in thought, had turned his horse's head.

"Call your brother Arthur," he said. "And, both of you, follow me."

In silence, he rode to the churchyard, and in silence, his two sons followed him. When they all dismounted near the stone Sir Hector looked at Arthur, who stood quietly by.

"Put the sword back again!" said he. And Arthur did so.

Sir Hector turned, then, to Sir Kay.

"Draw it out," he commanded. But Sir Kay, when he put his hand to the sword, could no

The Sword in the Great White Stone

more do this than any of the barons who had tried so hard.

Then Sir Hector himself tried, and also failed. Tenderly he laid his hand on Arthur's shoulder.

"It is your turn, now. Show me—show your brother—the truth!"

So Arthur, still quite simply and naturally, reached out his quick young fingers and, taking the sword for the second time from the shining white stone, would have given it into Sir Hector's hand. But Sir Hector, instead of taking the sword, bent on one knee and did Arthur homage, as all good knights do homage to their liege lord and King.

"My son," said he, "—and that I cannot help calling you, though you are not my son—the writing in the golden letters was set down on the marble slab for *you!* Hail! Arthur, son of Uther Pendragon, and King of Britain! Receive, before all others, the loyalty of those who love you best! Sir Hector, whom you have called 'father,' and his son, your brother, Sir Kay."

A Lady of the Lake

Everybody in Britain knew that the only son of Uther Pendragon had been found at last; and, though some of the barons were very angry, and refused at first to accept the "beardless boy," as they called him, they gave in when the beautiful Queen, Ygierne, openly declared him to be the child of the dead King and herself. So Arthur was crowned with great rejoicings and feastings, jousts and tournaments, which lasted for at least thirty days and thirty nights.

Never was there so handsome and so favored a young sovereign! Not only did all the knights and ladies of his court think the world of him, but the fairies of the forests and lakes loved him, too. Had he not been given into the special care of Merlin, that master of magic who knew a hundred times more secrets than the fairies knew themselves? Arthur's sister, too, was half a fairy, and was called *Morgan-le-Fey,* which means Morgan the fairy-maiden. She knew all sorts of spells, both good and bad, and could have told (only she never did) what sort of words to use if you wanted to get inside mountains, or down to the bottom of deep lakes; and how to get out of such places again, which, on the whole, was almost more important than how to get in. She could read stories in the stars, and tell you the wonderful enchantments that might, any moonlit night, be woven by means of a hazel wand, held in a certain very secret manner. She knew exactly what kind of fern seed would make you invisible, and where to find the flowers that were used for wonderful wine that smelt like cowslips and wild honey and made you fall head-over-heels in love! There was no end to Morgan-the-Fairy's magic, for, indeed, she was only a few degrees less clever than Merlin, the wizard, himself.

Arthur and his sister were very fond of each other, though, like a good many other brothers and sisters, they quarreled a little sometimes. It is, however, pretty certain that Morgan had something to do with the way in which the young King came into possession of a second sword, much more marvelous than the one which, before he was known as Uther's son, he had pulled out of the shining white stone in the churchyard to give to his brother, Sir Kay.

Not very far from Arthur's castle—which was at a place called Caerleon, quite a long way from Tintagel—a big wood grew, all dark and shady with pines and oaks. In the middle of the wood was a fountain, which was always full of clear spring water. By the fountain a beautiful tent ap-

A Lady of the Lake

peared one day, hung inside with satin curtains, and decorated with tassels of silver and gold. Just outside the tent a horse in bright, rich trappings was tethered; and on a bough over the horse's head hung a magnificent shield, set thickly with jewels and enameled in as many colors as a peacock's tail!

As soon as this lovely tent and horse and shield appeared by the side of the fountain, all the passers-by knew their meaning. Some strange and powerful knight from a distant country had taken up his post in the middle of one of King Arthur's private forests and was challenging anybody and everybody to come and turn him out! This was a thing that happened very often in those days; and there was never any lack of knights to answer the challenge. In fact, the whole court was generally delighted to hear of such a stranger. It meant honor and glory to every knight who rode out to do him battle, and great distinction to the one who succeeded in conquering him, and bringing him, a prisoner, to the throne of the King.

The first person to come and tell Arthur about the knight who had set up this beautiful tent by the fountain was a very brave youth called Griflet, who was only a page at the court of Caerleon. He begged the King to give him the order of knighthood, that he might ride off at once to the forest and fight with the stranger, who, he said eagerly, was one of the strongest, bravest, cleverest knights in the whole world. Arthur hesitated, for he thought Griflet was too inexperienced and young. But Merlin told him to do as the lad asked; so the King made him a knight as he asked, and, calling him "Sir Griflet" for the first time, made him promise to come back to the court if he failed in the brave deed he was so anxious to perform. Sir Griflet promised, and rode off. But in a few hours, he came riding back again, terribly wounded, and dreadfully unhappy and disappointed. The knight by the fountain had easily conquered him, and thrown both him and his horse to the ground. But instead of killing him there and then, the stranger had, himself, dismounted and given aid to poor Sir Griflet, telling him he was a brave youngster and would make a fine fighter when he was a little older. Then he had set the young knight on his horse again and sent him back to the King.

Well, when Arthur heard Sir Griflet's story, he exclaimed that the stranger was, indeed, a fine and generous knight, and that he would himself go off to the forest and challenge him to a battle! For, in those days, the more splendid and brave an enemy was, the more honor there was in fighting him. So off went King Arthur on a magnificent war-horse, the very best in his stable, his shield and sword and breastplate shining and his lord chamberlain, mounted on another fine horse, trotting a little way behind.

On the way, Merlin joined them, and walked by the King's stirrup, saying he thought he might be wanted before the day was over. As he and Arthur talked together, they came in sight of the richly-colored tent, with the strange knight, dressed in all his bright armor, standing by the side of the tree where his shield was hanging, its jewels and enamel gleaming in the shade of the boughs. When he saw another knight riding in the forest, he stepped forward and stood, very proud and upright, barring the way that led onward through the wood.

"How now!" cried Arthur. "Then no one may pass this way without a fight?"

"That is so," answered the knight, as bold and haughty as you please. "Are you ready?"

"Quite ready!" replied Arthur joyfully. "Mount your horse, and we will see which of us is the better knight."

So the stranger leaped upon his horse, and, with sword and spear, King and knight sprang toward each other to do battle. Such a crash rang through the forest as they met! If you heard it today, you would think some dreadful accident had happened! But the noise was only the noise of the King's spear striking the shield of the knight and the knight's spear striking the shield of the

King. And so vigorously did each strike that both the spears were shivered into a thousand pieces.

Then the lord chamberlain rode up with two new, unbroken spears, and the two brave warriors met again, with even a louder crash than before. Again, each spear was shattered to bits. By this time both King and knight were hot with battle, and, springing from their horses, they rushed at each other on foot, brandishing their sharp, shining swords. Over and over again, they struck, one at the other, each trying to strike the conquering blow. At last the stranger-knight drew back for a moment. King Arthur, thinking he was exhausted, leaped toward him. But the other suddenly swung his sword high above his head and brought it with all his force against the King's sword as Arthur made his spring. So violent was the knight's great blow that it cut right through the sword of the King, who was left with only the jagged handle in his grasp.

Then Arthur threw away the handle, and rushed to the knight with his mailed gloves. So they fought again, rocking and swaying together like two mighty wrestlers. And, at last, King Arthur was thrown to the ground and lay senseless among the bruised ferns and crushed wild flowers of the forest floor.

The stranger-knight lifted high his own unbroken sword to cut off the fainting King's head. But Merlin, who had been watching, sprang for-

A Lady of the Lake

ward and waved his wizard's wand. Instantly, the knight slipped slowly to the ground and lay beside the King in a deep sleep, while Merlin lifted Arthur and set him, only half-conscious, on the stranger's horse.

The King, pale and exhausted, looked down on the knight as Merlin led the horse away. "Oh, Merlin, Merlin!" he cried. "You have killed the finest knight that ever did battle against a King!"

"Not so!" answered Merlin. "He is only asleep, and it is a good thing for you he is not awake! But come! You must have another sword to make up for the one that has been broken in the fight!"

So on they went, through the trees, Merlin still leading the horse. Presently they came to a big, open space in the forest, and there, in the afternoon sunlight, glimmered the wide waters of a mysterious lake. Nothing and nobody was in sight—no cottages, no castles, no people, no wild foxes, or deer. But right in the middle of the lake, a white hand and arm were stretched out from the water, as motionless as if they were carved in ivory. A long sleeve of pearly satin was folded about the arm; and the hand held the most beautiful jeweled sword that Arthur had ever seen in his life.

As the King looked, amazed, he saw a fairy-maiden in a silver gown, with golden hair, walking on the green water just as a pretty girl might walk on a green meadow. She came stepping daintily toward them, and Arthur asked Merlin who she was.

"She is Nimue, the Lady of the Lake," said Merlin, "and, if you ask her, very courteously, she will tell you how to get the sword."

So, when the Lady of the Lake set her pretty little foot on the shore, Arthur went toward her and, bowing very low, asked her to tell him the way in which he could get the sword.

Then the maiden smiled, and showed him a fairy barge, hidden all among the reeds and rushes. She told him he had only to get into the barge and row himself into the middle of the lake and take the sword out of the fair white hand which held it. "And for my reward for telling you this," said she, "one day I will come to the court and claim a favor from you!" Then she disappeared, and Arthur and Merlin, springing into the barge, rowed out into the middle of the lake as fast as they could.

All this time, the hand and arm that held the sword had remained quite still. How strange they looked, rising so mysteriously from the quiet, glimmering water! How Arthur marveled, as he drew nearer and nearer, at the slim wrist, and the delicate fingers, of that strange white hand! What lady or fairy could it be who lived under the waves of that wonderful mere and was offering this beautiful jeweled gift to a human King?

The barge drew close up to the motionless arm; and Arthur, leaning over the side, put out his hand. Very gently and carefully, he drew the shining sword from the fairy fingers. As soon as he touched it, they released their clasp, and the arm went slowly, slowly down into the lake. The ripples closed over it with a little murmur, and it was gone.

Then Merlin rowed the barge back again to the rocky, reedy bank of the lake. The lady who had told them to take the sword was nowhere to be seen. She had disappeared entirely, leaving not so much as a glimmer of her silver gown, or a gleam of her golden hair, among the dark pines that grew right down to the water's edge.

Arthur and Merlin got out of the barge, and Arthur fastened the fairy sword to his side. Then Merlin, who had read all about it in one of his fairy books, told him that the sword was called "Excalibur," and that it was just as precious and wonderful as the Round Table itself. The wizard told the King, too, the name of the stranger-knight, which was Pellinore, and said that he, also, was a great King. But, when Arthur wanted to go and finish the battle with Pellinore—now that he had a fairy sword to fight with—Merlin said that he had fought quite enough for one day. So he and the King rode back to Caerleon with Excalibur hanging by Arthur's side; while King

Pellinore awoke quietly from his enchanted sleep and went to rest in his tent, hung with silken curtains and golden tassels, that he had set up by the side of the fern-fringed fountain in the shade of the forest trees.

The Princess Guinevere

King Leodogran, as you know, was an old friend of King Uther Pendragon, who had given him the charge of Merlin's wonderful Round Table, where seats could be found for two hundred and fifty knights. This Round Table was kept in the banqueting hall of Leodogran's big stone castle at Cameliard. All the knights who feasted there were under a vow; and the words of this vow were some of the noblest words that have ever been spoken in the history of the world. As well as the Round Table, Leodogran's castle held another great treasure—his only daughter Guinevere, the most beautiful and gracious maiden in the whole wide earth.

Guinevere flitted about the castle almost like a fairy princess, so golden was her hair, so blue were her eyes, so peach-pink her delicately rounded cheeks. Sometimes she sang to herself, softly, in the great hall; sometimes she sat in her bedroom window doing embroidery; sometimes she went to and fro among her maidens, overlooking them as they spun linen thread upon their pretty spinning wheels or wove the same thread into shining damask on their dainty looms. When her father's step was heard on the flags of the stone floors, Guinevere would lay everything aside and hasten to meet him. If he were tired and battle-worn—as often, indeed, she found him—she would bring him cool, clear water in a silver basin, place his hands in it, and dry them herself with a fine towel, before offering him a crystal goblet brimming with red wine to drink. Leodogran thought there was nobody like his daughter Guinevere, though he was silent and almost cold to her, and sometimes, even, very strict and stern.

One morning, the King of Cameliard, who had been away for some days, came galloping back to the castle on his war-horse, and cried to the servants to let down the portcullis—the great entrance door—to raise the bridge over the moat, and to prepare for a siege. His enemies were riding in hundreds over the near hills. The Knights of the Round Table came hurrying into the great hall, their pages running after them, to buckle on their masters' armor as fast as they could. But instead of a page, Leodogran was waited upon by his own daughter, the Princess Guinevere, who brought him his helmet, his breastplate, his sword, and his shield. Praying to heaven to protect him, she watched the King ride out of the courtyard at the head of his noble knights. Then she, herself, looked after the preparations for the siege of the castle before, running lightly up the winding stone stairs, she took up her stand by the window of a high tower, from which she could watch the battle.

What a clash of armies she saw outside! What waving of banners, galloping and rearing of horses, cries of triumph or despair! Here, there, and everywhere flashed Leodogran in his bright armor, supported always by the knights of the Round Table. For long they held their own, but by and by Princess Guinevere, gazing always from the window, felt her heart shaken with sudden fear. She saw the knights pressed hard on every side by an army stronger in numbers than themselves. They fought fiercely and magnificently, but they were being driven back toward the castle walls. Would they be able to drive away these eager and terrible regiments of foes? Or would they be forced to yield and give Cameliard into the hands of the enemy?

Princess Guinevere tried hard not to tremble, but she went numb and cold with dismay. Then, all at once, she heard a shout of encouragement and triumph. Down among her father's foes came riding an unknown knight, the noblest in bearing, the most beautiful in face, the brightest in armor that the Princess had ever seen. Above his head floated a banner which showed a Dragon wrought in gleaming gold! In his hand shone a sword of brilliant steel, its handle set thickly with diamonds, rubies, and pearls. Who was he, and whence could he have come?

Guinevere leaned far out of the casement, joyful and reassured, for the tide of battle immediately turned. In and out, backwards and forwards, glittered the golden sign of the Dragon, while the strange knight's sword flashed among the enemy like a flame. Whoever was touched by this sword, however lightly, fell from his horse to the ground. Its owner seemed to be everywhere at once. He had slain hundreds of Leodogran's enemies, when, quite suddenly, an old man appeared by his bridle and threw his war-horse back upon its haunches.

"Enough!" cried this old man—who had come from no one knew where—"Enough! Do you not see that the battle is won? The whole army of enemies is in flight!"

Then the stranger-knight paused and saw, indeed, a confused mass of men and horses riding fast for the distant hills. He bowed his head, and slowly pushed his sword into its sheath. Then up rode King Leodogran, grim, bloodstained and weary, and bent low in his saddle to the young brave stranger who had saved his castle and all that was in it.

"Beautiful and courageous knight!" said Leodogran. "How can I thank you? Come—follow me into my castle. I do not know who you are, but

you have saved my home for me, and anything or everything in it is yours for the asking."

The knight also bent low in his saddle, for the knights of those days were always very dignified and very courteous. Then the big portcullis was raised again, the bridge let down over the moat. Two and two, kings and knights, they all rode into the courtyard of the castle, and the sound of the horses' hoofs reached Princess Guinevere as she came hurrying down from the window of the high tower.

How busy everybody in the castle was, to be sure! Pages, with big baskets on their arms, were strewing the floors with bright fresh rushes, mingled with wild flowers. Cooks, in the kitchen, were roasting and stewing and baking with all their might. And delighted, smiling maidens were pouring cool scented water into basins, taking clean white towels out of the presses, and bringing soft rich robes into the big hall, ready to lay on the knights' shoulders when the pages had taken off the stained and heavy armor in which these brave gentlemen had fought.

King Leodogran led the stranger-knight to the seat of honor and bade him rest. As the tired soldier sank down upon a couch all clean and fresh with piles of sweet-smelling rushes, he saw a lovely lady coming quickly forward from among the sewing-maidens who were waiting on the knights of the Round Table. She wore the prettiest gold headdress, the daintiest silk gown in the world, and she carried her silver basin and white towel very carefully indeed. It was the Princess Guinevere, hastening to wait, courteously and lovingly, on her father, the King.

But as she curtseyed deeply to him, he waved her from him and pointed to his guest, who was watching earnestly from his couch of green rushes. "Wait, first, on the stranger-knight," said Leodogran. "Had it not been for his help, the castle of Cameliard would have fallen."

So Guinevere turned from her father to the stranger-knight. And the moment the eyes of the knight and the maiden met, the two fell in love.

How wonderful it seemed to both! The soldier in his armor looked adoringly at the sweet face under the golden headdress, the long hair, no less golden, which fell in two plaits to the very hem of this fair lady's gown. Guinevere, for her part, hardly lifted her shy blue eyes from the ground as she helped the stranger to take off his breastplate, laid a rich satin cloak on his shoulders, offered him the water and the towel, and called to a servant to bring a refreshing drink. The old man, who had entered the castle with the knights, smiled as he watched them, and, drawing near to Leodogran, pointed out the pretty sight.

"You offered anything your castle held to your deliverer," said he. "I think I know what gift your visitor will be asking soon!"

King Leodogran started, and looked rather dismayed.

"Who is he?" he asked. "And who, old man, are you?"

The King stared very closely at his unknown visitor, who only shook his head.

"No matter—no matter!" said he. "But what of your promise to give the knight anything he asks?"

"My promise shall be kept," said Leodogran proudly. And the old man smiled again as he stepped away.

Then everyone in the hall began to move toward the banqueting room, and the two hundred and fifty knights took their places at the Round Table, which was spread for a great feast. King Leodogran stood watching them; and the stranger-knight stepped forward and joined him, looking at him very earnestly indeed.

"Good and great King," said he, "I am from a distant court, and do not know your customs here. What is this Round Table, and who are these knights who have taken their places about it?"

Leodogran answered gravely:

"Brave stranger," he said, "that Round Table was left in my charge by a great King—Uther Pendragon himself. Whoever takes his place at it must share in a noble vow. Will you sit among my two hundred and fifty knights? Will you join in the words of the vow?"

The Princess Guinevere

The knight's face had become very bright and eager when he heard the name of Uther Pendragon. He looked to the right and saw the old man's eyes fixed earnestly upon him; he looked to the left and met the shy, gentle gaze of beautiful Guinevere. Then he made a quick step forward and took his seat at the table among the two hundred and fifty knights.

"Will you admit me to your fellowship?" he cried in a piercing voice. "Will you let me hear, and share, the words of your vow?"

Then all the two hundred and fifty knights sprang to their feet, and two hundred and fifty voices rang out in the great vow.

"To right the wrong, to punish the guilty, to feed the hungry, to help the feeble, to obey the law, and never to turn away from a woman in distress; this is the vow of the Knights of the Round Table!"

The sound of voices ceased, and everybody turned to the stranger, who had drawn his sword, and was holding it on high. Word for word, he repeated the vow in a ringing voice and then thrust his sword back into the scabbard, looking, with his whole heart in his eyes, at Princess Guinevere.

Leodogran stepped forward, and held up his hand for silence.

"Sir Knight," he said, "who are you?"

With a triumphant smile, the stranger answered him:

"I am Arthur, King of Britain, and proud so to be, but far, far prouder to have become a Knight of the Round Table—"

He paused for a moment, then moved swiftly forward and knelt on one knee before Guinevere as he finished speaking:

"And proudest of all, King Leodogran, to put my sword, my spear, my life, at the service of this fair and beautiful lady!"

Then the old man came toward them, and King Leodogran knew him for Merlin, the great magician. Merlin took Guinevere's hand and held it toward her father: and Leodogran placed it in Arthur's quick clasp, and raising him to his feet, bent very low before him.

"My liege and lord," said he, "I would have given my daughter willingly and gladly to the knight who saved Cameliard. How much more joyfully I give her to Arthur, son of Uther Pendragon, King of Britain, and Knight of the Round Table."

*The Empty Seat
at the Round Table*

One spring morning the sun rose, bright and beautiful, over the high towers of Camelot. The birds were singing among the apple-bloom; the oak trees were shaking out their little tufts of greeny-gold; the may blossoms were nodding their heads among the long grass all spangled with dew. Camelot was hung with banners and flags; its doors were decorated with silken curtains; and its pathways were arched with rainbows of flowers. Magnificent tapestries adorned the walls; fresh rushes, mixed with garlands, covered the stone floors. Everybody was running about with silver dishes and golden goblets, with cakes and fruit and honey and wine. For King Arthur's wedding day was close at hand, and Guinevere was on her way to Camelot with a train of ladies-in-waiting and a bodyguard of knights, bringing the Round Table that had been made by Merlin in imitation of the silver table brought so long ago by Joseph and the Rich Fisher to the country of West-over-the-Sea.

At this Round Table, as you know the young King had taken his knightly vow. How glad he was to think that it was to stand under the roof of Camelot, and that, sitting all about it, his fellow-knights would join in his wedding breakfast. He stood with Merlin in the great gateway of his royal castle, dressed in armor that shone like gold. All about him were his faithful courtiers waiting to greet the strangers who were coming from the court of Leodogran. The great company of the Round Table was to be completed today. Many knights had made the vow in times gone by; some had failed to keep it, and some had been killed in battle. But today, the day before Arthur's wedding, every seat was to be filled.

This was the King's purpose, as he waited at the entrance of his castle in his armor of gold. Presently, from the distance, came the murmur of a crowd, the tramping of horses' hoofs, and the roll of wheels. Over the hills toward Camelot poured the glittering procession of the royal bride—banners waving and minstrels singing stirring and noble songs. It was a magnificent sight; and no less magnificent was the sight that was waiting for the strangers in King Arthur's own splendid court.

His heart was beating fast with excitement and joy as the procession came along the meadow right up to the big castle gates. Arthur moved forward, and bent very, very low. For, on the leading horse, he saw his lovely lady, Guinevere, riding in royal dignity, a rich hood hiding her beautiful

The Empty Seat at the Round Table

golden hair, and an embroidered and jeweled cloak hanging from her slender shoulders. Close behind her rode her pages, ready to answer any call that she might give. Then came her ladies-in-waiting, each with a handsome knight in attendance. In the very midst of the procession marched a tall old man in white, crowned with mistletoe, and singing songs to the sound of a harp which he held in his hands; while a number of men followed just behind, carrying the Round Table!

King Arthur stepped forward and lifted Guinevere from her horse. Who knows what he did not whisper to her before he set her on the ground? Then he took her hand and led her forward, across the courtyard, between rows and rows of smiling, bowing attendants, right into the castle of Camelot, with the knights and ladies, who had come with her from her father's court, walking two-and-two behind.

A beautiful throne had been set high on a dais for the Princess, and Arthur led her up to it and saw her seat herself before he turned to welcome the noble company who followed. He bowed over the hands of the fair ladies; and all the knights bent, with stately courtesy, in greeting. The Round Table was brought in and put in the very middle of the hall. Arthur drew near and watched while his servants placed the seats about it; and, when they had set as many as it would hold, the King called to all the knights who belonged to the fellowship of the Round Table to gather round.

From among the brilliant company in the hall, a hundred knights stepped forward, all of whom had come with Princess Guinevere from the court of her father, King Leodogran. As they approached the Round Table, Arthur counted them over, one by one. When the hundred were complete, the King bowed to them once more. Then he turned to Merlin, who again stood beside him. Merlin took a roll of parchment from his pocket and began to read aloud from it.

He was reading the names of those among Arthur's own knights who had, for their courage and their goodness, their truth, charity, and uprightness, been considered worthy to join the noble fellowship of the Round Table. Some were old and scarred with battle; some were middle-aged; some were quite young, keen and vigorous to fight for honor and for the King. When the names rang down the hall they stepped forward, one by one. Bowing to Princess Guinevere as they passed the high dais, and to King Arthur as they reached him where he stood, they joined the hundred knights from the court of King Leodogran. Then the chief butler came forward with a great jeweled goblet in his hand, followed by two pages carrying golden jugs. The knights and the King took their seats at the table; the goblet was filled, and passing the jeweled cup from hand to hand, everybody drank to the fellowship of

knights good and brave and true—the great Fellowship of the Round Table.

All this time Guinevere watched, smiling and gracious, from her throne on the high dais. Her ladies-in-waiting were gathered about her, pretty as a big bunch of flowers. The knights looked at each other, and at the King, as they drank from the glittering cup; but they all rose to their feet and looked toward their future Queen, on her throne in the midst of them, as, at a sign from Arthur, their voices rang out, loud and glad and brave, in the words of the great vow.

The sound died away; and it was now the Princess Guinevere's turn to rise to her feet, sweet and fair and royal among them all. How proud and happy the King must have felt when he saw his lady standing among these bright and starry gentlemen, accepting their promise of chivalry with so delicate a grace! Her hair shone in the light from the high windows; her silk gown fell softly to her little slippered feet. She curtseyed very low to them all and waved her pretty white hands. Then she sat down again among her ladies; and, one by one, the knights of the Round Table stepped forward and, kneeling on one knee before Arthur, took the oath of loyalty to the King.

Merlin stood by, his roll of parchment, folded neatly up again in his hand. As each knight made his vow, the wizard bent his grave, wise head. But all the time, he was looking at the Round

The Empty Seat at the Round Table

Table. He seemed, as if in a dream, to see the vision of the Silver Table, and Joseph, and the Rich Fisher, and the Shining Cup that was called the Holy Grail.

Then, while he looked at the Round Table, he saw a mysterious thing happen. On all the seats that were placed about it letters of gold began to appear. They looked as if they were being written by invisible fingers holding an invisible pen. As Merlin watched, these letters grew bigger and brighter, so that they could be seen from quite a long way off. The old magician moved forward to read them more clearly; and when he stood quite close to the table, the wonder on his face changed into great gladness, for he knew that good spirits were in the banqueting hall, and that they had come from that mysterious, distant Fairyland where the Silver Table and the Shining Cup had been hidden so many, many years ago.

For what do you think had been written in each seat by the invisible fingers that held the invisible pen? Why, the name of the knight who had just risen from it to do homage to King Arthur, chief of them all. It was a sure sign to Merlin that the Round Table had been made by his own hands, for these very knights, and that their names were written also about the Silver Table which had been lost to men. He called to the King and to the Knights to come and read. They all gathered round, amazed, and spelled out the letters of their names; and then they took their places, shoulder to shoulder and hand to hand. But even as they did so, they saw that every seat was not yet filled. Two of them, one on Arthur's right hand, the other on his left, were still empty and unnamed.

Then King Arthur was very grieved and disappointed, for he had hoped that, today, the Fellowship of the Round Table would be quite complete. But Merlin had, all at once, seen into the future, and he knew the secret of those two empty seats. He laid his hand on the King's shoulder and consoled him.

"Be patient," said the magician. "Be patient! In one empty seat you will very soon see somebody whom you know and admire already, though, just now, I shall not tell you who he is! In the other, the Seat Perilous, no knight may sit today, nor tomorrow, nor for many years to come. And woe betide any knight who thinks that he may take his place at the Round Table in that place without a title! Look! See what is written there instead of a name!"

Arthur looked, and lo! he saw letters appear about the second empty seat, written, not in gold, but in flame! He read the words, marveling:

"I am the Seat Perilous."

Even as he finished reading the words, they faded away. But all the knights, and all the ladies, and Princess Guinevere herself, had seen the letters of flame. And right down the court ran the murmur of words:

"That empty seat is the Seat Perilous, and no knight may sit in it today, nor tomorrow, nor for many years to come!"

The Fairy Hunt

King Arthur and Princess Guinevere were married with great rejoicings, and all the barons and baronesses, the dukes and duchesses of the country came to the wedding. Such a banquet it was at Camelot! Such songs, and dances, and tournaments! The whole neighborhood seemed to ring with the mirth of it; with the shouts and laughter and delicate music of a hundred harps. Every evening the King and Queen sat at the windows of the castle, watching processions of knights with torches, winding in and out of the trees. Every morning the radiant pair came out together, smiling and beautiful, to walk or ride across the meadow, so that the whole world might see them. The Queen just moved along daintily and silently, but the King was always watchful and alert, ready to hear grievances or to grant favors, ready, even, to give the order of knighthood to the poor sons of laborers and cowherds if they could prove to him that they were as noble and valiant at heart as any gentleman of the land.

But a day came when Merlin told Arthur that the merriment and feasting must pause for a time, and that the King must meet his knights in sober and earnest talk, seated at the Round Table. So Queen Guinevere and all the ladies of the court swept and rustled away, in a stately procession, to the women's quarters in the castle; and the King and the knights sat down at the Round Table, and passed the cup of fellowship from hand to hand. Then Merlin said that today the empty seat at the King's left hand was to be filled—not the Seat Perilous, but the other place which had been left without a name. Everybody wondered who the chosen knight could be, and they all stood up and waited as the great wizard went out of the door of the banqueting hall to bring in the newcomer and present him to the King.

After a minute or two, the sound of a galloping horse was heard through the window—a strong, fast horse which came, with hoofs like thunder, over the drawbridge of the moat. A knight's armor clashed in the courtyard; a knight's small silken banner fluttered against the casement, Merlin's voice spoke a greeting; and deep, full, gay tones echoed in reply. Down the corridor tramped the heavy feet of the stranger, and in the doorway his form showed, tall and broad. Merlin took his hand and led him forward, and King Arthur gave a cry of amazement. For who do you think it was? Why, none other than King Pellinore, the knight who had set up his tent by the side of the woodland fountain, and who

The Fairy Hunt

had been left lying in an enchanted sleep the last time that Arthur had seen him!

But King Arthur was pleased—oh, very pleased indeed! He bore the other King no ill-will for having broken his own royal sword—and very nearly his own royal head as well—in their mighty battle among the forest trees. Stepping forward, he greeted his old enemy warmly, declaring that he was a right goodly and noble knight, worthy to become a member of the Round Table. Pellinore said, in reply, that he was proud of many things in his life, but never prouder than at this moment, when he stood in the halls of Camelot and received the greeting of Camelot's King. Then he bent on one knee before Arthur and took the oath of fealty; and Arthur, himself, raised him up and placed him in the seat at his left-hand side, while the jeweled cup was passed round again, and all the other knights drank joyfully to Pellinore, the latest, and almost the finest, comer to the Round Table.

And now Merlin made a sign to Arthur, and the King sprang to his feet and drew his sword from his scabbard. Everybody else did the same. There was a moment's pause, and then all the brave voices rang out together. Standing side by side, shoulder to shoulder, their unsheathed swords glittering, their heads high and erect, the knights of the Round Table thundered out the words of the Vow.

The sound of it was still in the air, and not one of the company had sheathed his sword again, when a great commotion arose under the windows of the castle! Hounds were baying, horns were blowing, and a little dog seemed to be barking with all its might! A long, long way off, horses might be heard galloping as well. But nobody could be quite sure of that, because, as they all stared at each other in great astonishment, the door of the banqueting hall suddenly burst open and a great pure-white stag, with branching horns and eyes like balls of flame, bounded into the room, its hoofs, which seemed to be made of silver, flashing and ringing among the green rushes on the stone flags of the floor.

No sooner had it leaped through the doorway than everybody saw that the little white dog, which had been making such a noise outside, was hard on the heels of this beautiful and mysterious deer. And following instantly came a pack of thirty couple of great black hounds, in full cry after the snow-white stag. But of followers and huntsmen there was not a sign. Only the sound of fairy horns blowing in the air, and the galloping of unseen horses very far away.

Around the big banqueting hall swept this strange hunt, which was, in very truth, a hunt from Fairyland. Just as the great white stag reached the place where a handsome young knight was sitting, the little dog sprang right up at it, so that the big, beautiful creature leaped almost over the young knight's head. This knight was called Sir Gawaine, and the stag knocked him clean over in its flight from the little dog and the baying pack of hounds. Such a noise there was in the banqueting hall! Sir Gawaine sprang up, quite bewitched, and, catching up the little dog, joined the hunt, not knowing that it was a fairy hunt and would lead him goodness knows whither! Away he ran out of the room and out of the castle, and, putting the little dog on his horse just as huntsmen always did, went galloping off after the snow-white stag, with the thirty couple of coal-black hounds galloping alongside. But no sooner was he gone out of the door than a beautiful maiden, on the prettiest white pony you ever saw, came in at another, and rode right into the middle of the hall, and, pulling up her dainty steed, called to King Arthur to go after Sir Gawaine and to bring back the little fairy dog which he had stolen!

"The little dog is mine!" cried this beautiful unknown lady, "The knight had no business to take it away! Remember the Vow, King Arthur, remember the Vow! I am a lady in distress, and, as such, you have sworn to help me!"

King Arthur sat silent, his hand on his sword, and his eyes cast down. The Vow had seemed to him such a beautiful, serious thing, and he could not believe that it had anything to do with this wild fairy hunt, and this strange fairy lady, who certainly was not made of flesh and blood, but belonged to some enchanted forest a very long way off. He heard the noise of the black hounds and of Sir Gawaine's horse and of the little mysterious elfin dog fade in the distance among the faintly blowing horns of the invisible company; and he had not the slightest wish to go after them. He wanted to stay soberly in his royal castle with his beautiful royal bride.

As he hesitated, another startling and quite unexpected visitor came loudly in through the wide-open door. This time, it was a strange, shadowy knight almost as big as a giant, dressed in black armor and riding a huge black horse. He trotted up to the lady and, without a word to anybody, seized her pretty white pony by the bridle. Then he wheeled his horse about and rode quickly out of the door again, leading the lady's pony, and taking no notice of her cries and tears. It all happened so quickly that not a single knight of the Round Table had time to spring to the lady's rescue, nor even to see the face of the shadowy knight in the black armor on the great black horse.

As they all stood, breathless and amazed, King Arthur suddenly found his voice and cried aloud, in ringing tones, to Merlin, the magician:

"Tell me, O great wizard," he cried, "what is the meaning of all this magic? Where did the fairy

The Fairy Hunt

stag and the fairy hounds and the fairy lady and the shadowy black knight come from? Was it not from your own Enchanted Forest where stands the perilous castle in the middle of the Valley of No Return?"

Merlin, whose face had been hidden under his magician's hood, suddenly flung away the covering. Everybody saw him, for a moment, as an old man, with a long white beard, wearing a crown of mistletoe. But even as they looked, his face changed. He seemed young, and very beautiful, and the crown of mistletoe became a laurel wreath on his hair, which was golden and like a boy's. His voice, when he answered Arthur, somehow reminded the King of the invisible fairy horns which they had all heard and which, no doubt, had called Sir Gawaine after them.

"And what if the hunt is only a fairy hunt and the lady only a fairy lady?" cried Merlin in this new, mysterious, silvery sort of voice. "Are you not brave enough to follow them into Fairyland? Is all your life going to be spent in royal castles, eating and drinking at rich banquets, listening to the music of golden harps, and meeting other knights in mock battles, with swords and shields? Do you not know what high adventure means? If not, I can soon tell you! It means the adventure of bright dreams, and of lovely visions, and of things that are only very dimly seen and heard. Follow the Fairy Hunt, good King Arthur! Go after the vision of the snow-white stag and the sweet, sorrowful lady and the dark knight! What if she has only asked you to bring back her little white dog? What if you think it is all magic mixed with folly and you would be better staying quietly at home? Have the kingly courage to take horse and to follow Sir Gawaine into Fairyland—to storm the doors of the Castle Perilous and to brave the darkness of the Valley of No Return!"

Then Arthur drew himself erect, and King Pellinore sprang to his feet at the King's right hand. "I, too, am a King," cried Pellinore. "I, too, am of royal blood! It is for kings to lead the way into the mysterious places of which the great wizard has spoken. Come, King Arthur! We will set off on this high adventure together!"

"You say well!" cried Merlin. "You say well! You have your own good sword, King Pellinore! You have used it well and strongly more than once. Use it well and strongly again! And for you, my own great sovereign, my dearly loved Arthur, you have Excalibur! Excalibur, which you took from the hand that held it high above the enchanted lake! Carry Excalibur with you and use it, always, to defend the right. Then you need not fear the places of dark spirits and of old, unhappy witcheries! Forward, forward, both of you! Go, like brave and chivalrous Kings, into Fairyland! What you will see and find there will be your high and beautiful reward!"

The Fairy Hunt

Merlin finished speaking and folded his hood once more about his face and hair. King Arthur and King Pellinore went out of the banqueting hall and sprang each upon his own war-horse. Then off they went, side by side, after the fairy hunt, while Merlin, hidden in his hood, passed away from the sight of the knights of the Round Table. Where he went to, none of them knew, very likely back to his own home in the forest— the home in which he had once seen the vision of Joseph, and the Rich Fisher, and the Holy Grail.

Merlin knew that, one day, King Arthur, and King Pellinore, and all the knights of the Round Table would see the vision, too, but that this would only be when they had passed through the dangers of the Enchanted Forest, and stormed the Castle Perilous, and gone, without losing themselves entirely, through the valley that was called the Valley of No Return.

King Pellinore's Adventure

King Pellinore, that big knight who once nearly killed King Arthur and then took a place at the Round Table and made the great Vow, had many adventures in his day, but the one you are going to hear about was the greatest of all. You remember that he had galloped off at full speed after the Fairy Hunt. As he galloped, he swore to himself that he would save the pretty, weeping lady who had been carried off by the Black Knight, and would either bring her back in safety to Arthur's court, or would wander in the Enchanted Forest for the rest of his life. He had become separated from King Arthur, and was now quite alone among the trees of this strange place; but, just in front of him, he could still hear the baying and yelping of the sixty coal-black hounds.

He rode on as fast as he could, and then something happened that would have amazed another knight, but did not surprise King Pellinore at all, because he had known such a thing to happen before. The baying of the hounds suddenly went all muffled and strange, as if they had disappeared inside a cave. The King turned the corner; and there, in front of him, stood a great beast that was not like a lion, nor a bear, nor even a dragon, nor anything in the world except itself. It stood and glared at him before turning around and lumbering away, crashing through the undergrowth with as much noise as a hippopotamus. And through the mouth of the beast, there still came the muffled baying of the hounds. This strange monster had swallowed them all, but they seemed still to be hunting the fairy stag in the very middle of the beast's inside!

King Pellinore gave a great shout, for he had been hunting this beast all his life, and knew he would probably go on hunting it until he died, and never be able to kill it, after all! But meanwhile, he followed it hard through bush and brier, often losing sight of it, but always hearing the strange, muffled music of the fairy hounds. At last, the beast disappeared altogether, and he saw a lady sitting by a fountain, who showed him the path through the Enchanted Forest that he must take, and told him that already the Black Knight and the pretty, weeping maiden had gone that way. So then King Pellinore knew that, in following the beast, he had come in the right direction for the fulfillment of his vow.

He heard the hounds still baying, but a long, long way off, as he hurried down the path shown him by the lady. In a very few minutes, he reached a clearing in the wood where two beautiful tents, one blue and one crimson, were set up opposite each other in the flickering lights and shadows of the trees. At the door of one of these tents stood the maiden he had come to save; and on the trodden grass in the middle of the clearing, the Black Knight, on the black horse, was doing battle with sword and shield against another knight who seemed almost as big and strong as his enemy.

King Pellinore poised his spear in his raised hand and, galloping forward, drove his way between them. "How, now?" he cried. "How is this? Who are you both, that you fight in this way for the lady yonder, who belongs to neither of you, but came of her own will to ask the protection of King Arthur?"

The Black Knight had pulled his great horse onto its haunches, but he shouted back at King Pellinore, whom he did not know as one of the knights of the Round Table.

"The lady is mine!" cried the Black Knight. "This foolish fellow, here, is trying to steal her from me. But she is mine! I fought King Arthur for her, and I conquered him!"

"That is not true!" shouted King Pellinore—and his voice rang all through the forest in its anger. "I was there and I saw it all! You carried the lady away before a single knight of the Round Table had time to spring to arms and do battle for her. But every man of Arthur's court knows you have no right to her! I have followed the coal-black hounds, and the beast which swallowed the hounds, all the way through this Enchanted Forest to take the lady back again! Come! Meet me here in this open space of grass, and we will soon see which is the better man."

Then the Black Knight rushed upon King Pellinore, and with their swords and shields and spears they fought until the forest rang with the noise. But the King was soon the conqueror. He killed the Black Knight's horse, and when he saw his enemy lying on the crushed turf, he also sprang to the ground, to finish the fight fairly on foot. And finish it he did, for he cut off the wicked Black Knight's head.

Then the other knight, who had watched the battle from a little distance, came forward gladly and told King Pellinore to take the lady back to Arthur's court. "I was but trying to save her from the Black Knight," he said. "I knew that he had no right to her!" And he brought out a fresh, strong horse that had been tethered to a tree and put King Pellinore's saddle and bridle upon it, and said he would care for the tired, hot horse which had been in the battle. After which, he went up to the door of the tent and, giving his hand to the lady, led her forward.

The lady had stopped crying now, and had let down her long veil and wound her hood about her head, so that King Pellinore could not see her face. He lifted her into the saddle before springing up in front of her; and he thought that she felt a sweet, small, cool thing, and that she smelled of wild roses and violets washed in dew. How lightly she seemed to sit behind him, too! His big horse took no count of her extra weight as it trotted off through the trees, where the night shadows were gathering and the stars already twinkling high up among the boughs.

On and on rode King Pellinore and the lady, until it was quite dark. Then he stopped his horse and lifted her down, and they slept under the trees. He was almost surprised to see in the morning that she was still there, because he guessed she was more than half a fairy and not made like other ladies he had known. When they rode on again, and passed out of the Enchanted Forest, he wondered if she would take wing, like a moth or a butterfly, and remain behind! But she did not, and when the sun was high in the sky, both King and lady rode safely into the courtyard of the castle at Camelot.

Then King Arthur, and Sir Gawaine, who having soon lost the sound of the Fairy Hunt had returned without encountering any adventures worth recording, and all the rest came out to meet them, and welcomed the lady right gladly, and gave praise and honor to King Pellinore. But the lady was still veiled; and at last, King Arthur turned to her with courtesy.

"You will find shelter and happiness forever

at my court," said he. "The knights of the Round Table will be at your service always—ready to protect you and never failing to honor you. But you came and went almost as swiftly, and with as much surprise to us, as the Fairy Hunt itself—to which, somehow, I think you half belong. Will you, then, let us now see your face?"

Then the lady threw back her veil and hood, and showed her pretty face, quite radiant, to the King and all his knights. The knights murmured in admiration, for she was very beautiful. But the King cried out with joy, for he knew her, now, as he had not known her when the Black Knight carried her away.

"You are sweet Nimue!" he exclaimed. "You are she who showed me the barge in which I rowed to take my sword Excalibur from the hand that held it above the water! You are one of those wonderful beings who love the world of knighthood—one of the Ladies of the Lake!"

Nimue smiled, and let her veil fall again, before she answered:

"Yes, I am Nimue, a Lady of the Lake!" said she. "And you have fulfilled your promise to me, King Arthur! From today I shall never be far away from you. With the other ladies, my fairy-friends, I will come and go between the Enchanted Forest and the royal and knightly court of Camelot."

Sir Gawaine's Adventure

You remember that Sir Gawaine had been the first of the knights of the Round Table to leap upon his horse and follow the Fairy Hunt. Perhaps because he was the first to ride away into Fairyland, he had, at one time, the most marvelous adventure that befell any knight in those wonderful days of romance.

It all came about through another knight, Sir Kay, who told a story of a hidden fountain which, he said, was to be found over the waters of the sea, bubbling up among the mosses in the very heart of another enchanted forest called Broceliande. There were strange tales related of this fountain—of its magical waters, its ferny secrets, the mysterious white marble slab upon its brink, and the fairy birds that sang in the blossoming thorn trees set round about it. Whoever could make his way to the fountain would be sure of the finest adventure in all the world.

When Sir Gawaine heard about the fountain, and the promised adventure, he did not hesitate a moment. He took ship to Brittany, and took his horse and his armor with him. When he landed, he mounted and rode away over the moors and through the villages until he reached Broceliande. The enchanted part began in a valley, which was the loveliest valley in the world. Every kind of wild flower grew there and a sparkling stream splashed and bubbled among the sunlit stones. Sir Gawaine followed the stream until he reached a castle which shone like silver and had all its bright towers reflected in a waterfall just below it. Two beautiful boys stood at the door of this castle, dressed in yellow satin, with gold crowns on their heads and gold shoes on their feet, gold daggers in their belts and white ivory bows in their hands. When the sound of Sir Gawaine's horse traveled up to the castle windows, a tall man, also dressed in yellow satin, came out of the door and advanced to meet the visitor, and Sir Gawaine, springing from his horse, bowed very low indeed, for he knew that the adventure had begun.

The man in the shining robe led Sir Gawaine into the castle, where twenty-four maidens sat in a row, embroidering twenty-four beautiful cloths. Six of them took Sir Gawaine's horse, six carried off his armor to wash it, and six took away his travel-stained clothes and brought him a robe, silk-lined, shining, and soft. The remaining six waited on him with silver bowls full of clear water and fine damask towels of green and white. Then they spread a delicious feast for him, and the man

Sir Gawaine's Adventure

in yellow satin asked him where he was going.

When Sir Gawaine replied that he was going to the magical fountain in search of high adventure, the man in yellow satin seemed delighted to have met so brave a knight. He ordered Sir Gawaine's horse to be brought around and showed him the path that would take him where he wished to go. Sir Gawaine rode off bravely in his bright, freshened armor and presently came to a sheltered glade, with a mound in the middle of it, where an enormous black man sat, with only one eye set right in the middle of his forehead, and who held an iron club in his right hand.

Around this ugly black giant stood a thousand wild animals—stags and boars, lions and tigers, serpents and dragons! Sir Gawaine was very much startled, but he spurred his horse on through the crowd of fierce, growling beasts, and riding straight up to the one-eyed black giant with the club, asked him as boldly as you please the way to the fairy mountain where a wandering knight could find the highest of all high adventures.

The great black giant scowled at him with his one eye, but answered the question. If Sir Gawaine would ride a little farther down the valley, he would see, presently, the tallest, greenest tree he had ever seen in his life. Under this tree bubbled the fountain; and by the side of the water was a white marble slab. On the slab was set a bowl of silver, fastened with a silver chain. Any knight who was brave enough to fill the silver bowl with water from the fountain, and then to pour the water over the white marble slab, would soon find himself in the middle of an adventure surprising and dangerous enough to satisfy the most courageous man in the world.

All this the giant growled out unwillingly, and the animals around him growled to keep him company. Sir Gawaine was not at all sorry to leave them and to ride forward among the shady oaks and pines. Presently he saw the tall and beautiful green tree of which the big black man had spoken —and there, at its foot, half-hidden by feathery ferns and plumy meadowsweet, were the white marble slab, the silver bowl, and the glimmering water of the fairy fountain.

Sir Gawaine dismounted and, without a moment's hesitation, took the silver bowl, filled it with water, and poured the water right over the white marble. In an instant, almost before he could spring on his horse again, the sky went as black as night, a clap of thunder shook the valley, and a hailstorm came beating and rattling about the tall green tree. Every leaf of the tree was beaten off, and then the storm passed and the sun came out again. And behold! instead of putting out fresh leaves, the tall tree seemed to blossom into hundreds and hundreds of little birds, which sat singing more sweetly and exquisitely than the sweetest, most exquisite music Sir Gawaine had ever heard!

Then, as he sat on his horse, entranced, a loud, deep wailing traveled along the valley, and down through the sunlight galloped a knight, who was the blackest of all the black knights ever seen before. He and his horse were like jet; his armor was like ebony. He wore a black velvet mask and carried a black linen pennon upon his lance. And he rushed upon Sir Gawaine, who spurred his horse to meet the other with a loud, defiant cry.

For many minutes they fought beside the fairy fountain, and then Sir Gawaine gave the Black Knight a mortal blow. But he did not fall at once —he only turned his horse's head and galloped away, with Sir Gawaine after him. In a short time, the high walls of a palace showed through the trees. The Black Knight galloped across the drawbridge and through the lifted iron gate. But, when Sir Gawaine would have followed, the great gate slid down between the high walls again and shut him out.

Sir Gawaine, disappointed, got down from his horse and peeped through the bars. And, to his surprise, he met the gaze of a charming maiden with curly golden hair who, as he was peeping in, was, in the same way, peeping out!

"Who are you?" said she. "And what do you want?"

"I want to come inside!" cried Sir Gawaine.

"This is, I know, my particular Palace of Adventure! Let me in, I pray you, to finish what I have begun!"

The maiden nodded her head quite kindly.

"I have been waiting here for you a long time," said she. "I always knew you would come! But I cannot let you in for all the world to see! Take this ring. Put it on your finger and you will be invisible, and then I will lift up the gate!"

So Sir Gawaine put on the ring and became invisible, and she lifted up the gate and admitted him. He went inside, leaving his horse to feed on the nice fresh grass without. The maiden, who, he saw now, was dressed in pretty boy's clothes, like a page, bade him follow her, keeping his hand upon her shoulder, for not even she could see him while he wore the ring. She led him to a wonderful gilded and painted chamber where he took off the ring, while the maiden kindled a fire, spread a silver table with golden plates, and gave him a delicious supper. When he had finished, she bade him listen to sounds of wailing that were coming up from below.

"The lord of the castle is dead!" said she. "He was the Black Knight of the Fountain, and has died from your blow. But it was always told that his lady should marry one of Arthur's knights. You must be he."

"Yes, I must be he!" cried Sir Gawaine. "This

is my high adventure, I know. Fair maiden, let me see the lady!"

"Peep through that little grating and you will see her in the hall below," said the maiden, preparing to clear away the golden plates and dishes.

So Sir Gawaine peeped, and, down in the hall, in a lovely black-and-silver gown, he saw a most beautiful lady sitting with candles all about her. She was pale and grave, but not very sad. She had never really loved the lord of the castle, but had, long ago, married him so that he might defend the fairy fountain, which belonged to her. Her name had always been the Lady of the Fountain, and she knew that she must marry again, immediately, so that those magical waters, that white slab with the silver bowl, that tall green tree might still be kept unhurt in the secret fairy places of Broceliande.

She sat among her tall lighted candles, her head on her hand. Sir Gawaine, watching her, felt his love for her spring up like a flame. He turned to the pretty maiden in the page's dress.

"I love the Lady of the Fountain!" he cried. "I have always loved her in my dreams! Take me to her."

"Tomorrow!" said the maiden. "I will take you tomorrow. Be assured she will love you in return. I think that she, too, has always known you would come!"

So the next day, the maiden gave Sir Gawaine a

beautiful robe to wear, with golden clasps in the shapes of lions. He looked right royal in it as he strode down the corridors of the castle into the presence of the Lady of the Fountain, who was sitting without any candles this morning, thoughtful and all alone. The maiden led Sir Gawaine to her, and she turned her beautiful pale face to him as he knelt silently on one knee before her.

"You?" she said. "Then it was you who fought with the Black Knight of the Fountain and killed him, so that he lies dead."

"It was my adventure, lady," said Sir Gawaine, softly. "He was only set to guard the fountain while you waited for me!"

The Lady of the Fountain made a sign to the pretty maiden who was dressed like a page.

"Call my nobles," said she. "I must speak with them."

Then, when all the nobles came, she pointed to Sir Gawaine, who was adoring her with his eyes.

"He has shown himself the strongest knight we have ever known," said she. "Tell me—for it is for you to decide—shall he guard the waters of the fairy fountain for me, and for all of you?"

The nobles, who knew that Sir Gawaine had conquered in a fair fight, said that he should. And then the lady stood up on her raised throne, walked down the steps, and gave Sir Gawaine her hand.

"Be it so!" said she. "Be faithful in your charge, Sir Gawaine, and keep the fairy fountain and the tall green tree safe under the sun, the rain, and the stars forever!"

Sir Tristram's Adventure

Sir Tristram was born in a country called Lyonnesse, and his mother was a great Queen, who died when he was only a few hours old. After some years, the King, his father, married again and had more children—handsome little sons and pretty little daughters. But their mother, Tristram's stepmother, was very jealous of the Prince, who was the child of her husband's first wife, and she tried to poison him. When the King found this out, he was very angry and ordered the wicked stepmother to be burned. But little Tristram burst into tears when he was told of this terrible punishment. He ran to the King, his father, and, kneeling at his feet, begged and prayed that his stepmother's life should be spared. So the King pardoned her, although he could never love her again. But good, forgiving little Tristram was always kind to her, and, after he had saved her life, the stepmother simply worshiped the ground upon which the young Prince trod.

He was brought up chiefly in Brittany, and then, when he had grown into a young man, he went to the court of King Mark of Cornwall. There, everybody liked him, and admired him heartily for his courage and his goodness of heart. He was musician as well as knight, and played the harp as beautifully as any minstrel, so that all the ladies of the court would sit together and whisper about him. They wished he would fall in love with one of them, but although he was the very soul of courtesy and chivalry, he had no desire to marry any lady of the land.

After a time, he went, as did all young knights in those days, to King Arthur's court and became a knight of the Round Table, while still quite young. He fought in many tournaments, and the ladies who watched would say to one another: "Here comes Sir Tristram. See the lions upon his shield!" For the lions were Sir Tristram's coat of arms, as they had been that of his father and his grandfather before him.

Then came a day in Sir Tristram's life which was very wonderful, and yet, in the end, very sad. He was sent to Ireland by King Mark, to bring back a beautiful Princess called Iseult, who was to be King Mark's bride, and take her place as Queen of Cornwall. Sir Tristram set off in a beautiful ship, with shining sails and cabins fitted up in silver and gold. He took his harp with him, and also his shield, his spear, his helmet, and his sword. He did not know whether there might not be many adventures waiting for him in Ireland,

and he wanted to be ready for anything that should happen.

Sure enough, no sooner did he reach Ireland than he found the King, Princess Iseult's father, in great need of help from the attacks of many enemies. So Sir Tristram put his sword and spear at the King's service and helped him in many a fight, until the Princess Iseult began to think that the young knight who had come to fetch her to Cornwall was the finest knight in the world. She used to take his shield and rub it bright for him, and admire the three lions, and say that Sir Tristram of Lyonnesse was, indeed, as brave as a lion himself. So that when at last they set sail together for Cornwall, after the King of Ireland had conquered his enemies, the two young people were more than half in love with each other.

But Princess Iseult would have married King Mark, and probably forgotten Tristram, if it had not been for something that happened on the voyage. You must know that Iseult had taken her lady-in-waiting with her, and that the Queen of Ireland had given this lady a magic drink in a crystal bottle with a gold stopper. It was a love-drink, a fairy wine, which would make those who drank it together love each other forever and ever, and care nothing for anybody else. This love-drink, said the Queen, was to be drunk by Iseult and King Mark on their wedding day.

Well, the weather was hot, and the sparkling

Sir Tristram's Adventure

sea seemed to make it hotter, and Sir Tristram sat on the deck of the fine ship in the sunshine and played his harp to beautiful Iseult. When he laid it down, she asked him to go into the cabin below and bring her something to drink, for she was very thirsty indeed with the warmth of the afternoon.

Sir Tristram went down, and there, on the table, he saw a pretty crystal bottle with a gold stopper, filled with what looked like sparkling wine. He carried it on deck to Princess Iseult, who took it eagerly into her hand, drew out the gold stopper, and tasted the fragrant drink. It gave her a delicious cool feeling, and she passed the crystal bottle to Sir Tristram and bade him also drink some. He did so—and then they looked at each other in amazement and rapture. They had drunk the fairy drink together, the drink which had been intended for Iseult and King Mark upon their wedding day.

Sir Tristram did not speak, but he took up his harp, and he played and sang the most beautiful and yet the saddest love-song that was ever composed. Iseult sat with her lovely face hidden in her white hands, and her dark hair shining like polished ebony in the sunlight. The breeze rustled mournfully in the sails of the ship, and the waves had a sorrowful sound in them, as if the very mermaids and water nymphs were weeping for poor young Sir Tristram and sweet Princess Iseult.

For never, never had two lovers felt love like that which had been hidden in the fairy drink, and which could not end in a happy mariage, because Iseult was the promised bride of King Mark.

So Tristram took his dear Princess to Cornwall, and she was married with royal rejoicings, and her sorrowful knight went away and had many great and fine adventures for her sake. But they could never forget what they had felt when they drank the fairy drink, and they were faithful to each other's memory until they died. And some people will tell you that they died on the same day, and that their bodies were laid side by side, and that out of their graves grew two fair climbing roses, which waved, all mixed together, in the sunshine, and dropped red and white petals to mingle, softly, upon the mossy ground.

The Pig-Sty Prince and the Many Travels

One of King Arthur's cousins was a little Prince who had been found in a pig-sty. The swineherd who found him, however, knew well enough that he was a Prince, and took him up to the King's palace, where, after a little time, the King acknowledged him as heir to the kingdom. The Prince's own mother was dead, but his stepmother, who was very fond of him, was determined that he should marry well. When he was grownup, therefore, she told him that only one Princess in the world was worthy of him, and that was the Princess Olwen.

The Pig-Sty Prince (everybody knew him by this name) immediately determined to marry the Princess Olwen, and set off to King Arthur's court to ask him for her hand as a kingly favor. For, in those days, anybody who wanted anything hurried off to ask King Arthur to give it to him. The Prince rode on a fine black horse, with a saddle and bridle of crimson and gold. When he reached King Arthur's palace the doorkeeper thought he had never seen so fine a man, and admitted him almost immediately. The Pig-Sty Prince begged the

King to give him the hand of the Princess Olwen, and the King said he would gladly have consented had he ever heard of her. As he had not, he sent out messengers who spent twelve months in looking for her, but were no wiser on the last day of the year than they had been on the first. In great disappointment, the Pig-Sty Prince called King Arthur a promise-breaker, and said he would go home, taking the king's honor with him.

But this could not be allowed. King Arthur was too great a King to permit even a Pig-Sty Prince to go home disappointed and empty-handed. He summoned the bravest and strongest of his knights and warriors, and bade them set off with the Prince in search of the Princess Olwen. So this wonderful band of strong and brave men rode away into the country; after some weeks of traveling, they saw a great castle in the distance. Just as they arrived within call of it, they came upon an immense flock of sheep in charge of a shepherd; so they rode up to him and asked him to whom the castle belonged. He answered that it belonged to the father of the Princess Olwen.

Then these warriors from Arthur's court said that they had come to take the Princess Olwen to the King. Whereupon, the shepherd told them that other strong and brave men had gone into the castle on the same quest, but that none had come out alive. He told them, too, that he was the brother of the lord of the castle, who had stolen all his possessions from him and made him shepherd of the castle sheep. Then the Pig-Sty Prince gave him a ring, which the shepherd took home and showed to his wife, who was very much pleased and excited, for the ring was a family treasure, and she knew, by what her husband told her, that her own sister's son was near at hand. As she was talking to the shepherd about the ring, all King Arthur's messengers rode up to the house, with the Pig-Sty Prince in the middle of them. The shepherd's wife greeted them, and showed great joy at meeting with her nephew. They all sat down to supper, and directly afterwards, the woman opened a big stone chest and out of it stepped a curly-headed boy. He was, she explained, the only son left to her out of twenty-four. The cruel lord had killed all the other twenty-three, and she was obliged to hide this one in the chest to keep him safe. Which shows what a dreadful man the father of the Princess Olwen must have been.

Then the shepherd's wife told her visitors that sometimes the Princess Olwen came to the cottage to wash her beautiful auburn hair, and that if a message was sent to her, she might come that very night. So a message was sent, and, sure enough, the Princess came. Her hair was indeed beautiful, and her skin was as white as the petals of the wood-anemones. She wore a white dress adorned with medallions of apple-green, and her flowing sleeves were apple-green also. And wherever she stepped four white clover-heads grew.

The moment that the Pig-Sty Prince saw her, he recognized her, and fell even more deeply in love with her real self than he had been with the image of her in his fancy. She, too, fell in love with him, but told him she was afraid he could never win her. His only chance, she said, was to ask her father for her hand, and to promise to perform every task which the cruel lord should command. Then she mounted her beautiful white pony and went back to the castle, accompanied for the first half of the way by the Pig-Sty Prince. King Arthur's messengers, who followed behind, remarked what a handsome pair they made.

The lord of the castle was a terrible-looking man, almost hidden in his own wild, long hair. Three times he tried to drive Arthur's messengers away with poisoned arrows, but each time they caught the arrows and flung them back at the lord. So at last—as he was very badly hurt by the arrows—he bade them declare their desire.

Then Arthur's warriors put the Pig-Sty Prince in a chair opposite the great chair in which sat the cruel lord. And the two began to argue, one against the other.

"You must root up the whole of that hill yonder," said the father of Princess Olwen; "you must plough it and sow it in one day, and in one day the wheat must grow and ripen. Of that wheat,

only, shall bread be baked for my daughter's wedding. All this must be done in one day."

"It will be quite easy for me to do this, though you may think it difficult," answered the Pig-Sty Prince, remembering what Olwen had told him about promising to do all that he was asked, though he saw very little chance of keeping his word.

"This may be easy, but there are other things which you cannot do. Only two men in the world can till the land and rid it of its stones. Neither of these will come for you, and you will not be able to make them. Another man has in his possession the only oxen that can possibly draw a plough over such wild country. He will not give them up to you, and you will not be able to get them. When first I met Olwen's mother, nine bushels of flax were sown, and from the seed not a blade came up. I require you to recover the flax and to sow it again in the wild land tilled by the men who will not come, and ploughed by the oxen you cannot get. When the flax has grown it must make the linen for the headdress my daughter is to wear at her wedding."

"It will be perfectly easy for me to do all these things," cried the Pig-Sty Prince valiantly. "Although you do not think that it is easy!"

"You may be able to sow the flax and to reap it in time for the linen headdress to be made which my daughter is to wear at her wedding," said the lord of the castle, "but there are other things you certainly cannot do. Yet I require that they be done. I want honey that is nine times sweeter than comb-honey, to put into the marriage-drink, and I must have the famous cup of which so many stories are told, to hold this sweet draught of wine. Then I will eat out of no dish at the wedding supper, but only out of the basket of plenty, into which any man in the world may dip his hand and bring out the food he likes best. Also, you must bring me the fairy horn, and the fairy harp, and the fairy cauldron of which all the world has heard tell. The fairy horn will pour out the wine, the fairy harp will play without a musician, and in the fairy cauldron meat may be boiled without a fire. Then I must certainly wash my head and shave my beard for the ceremony, and I can only shave with the great boar's razor. Nor can I spread out my hair in order to wash it unless I have blood from the jet-black witch."

"All these things I can easily get for you," boasted the Pig-Sty Prince, looking severely at the lord's extremely matted and untidy beard and hair.

"I shall want fresh milk, too, for some of my guests, and nobody has ever yet been able to carry fresh milk into the castle. It always turns sour. There are some magical bottles in which it can possibly be kept sweet, but it is impossible for you to find them."

"I will find the magical bottles and bring the milk," cried the Pig-Sty Prince, very loudly and firmly.

"Yes, but, even if I wash my head, my hair is so thick and matted I can only comb it with the fairy comb, and cut off the ends with the fairy scissors, that hang between the two ears of the great enchanted boar who also carries the razor."

"It will be perfectly easy for me to hunt the great enchanted boar and bring you the comb and scissors as well as the razor," shouted the Pig-Sty Prince at the top of his voice.

"In order to do so, you will want the fairy hound, and the fairy leash to hold him, and the fairy collar and chain, and the great huntsman whose name is Mabon, who was stolen from his mother when he was three days old and has been lost ever since. Whatever else you can do you certainly cannot find Mabon."

"It will be the easiest thing in the world for me to find Mabon. What else is there for me to do?" demanded the persistent lover of the Princess Olwen.

It appeared that there were various other things for him to do, one of which was to persuade King Arthur to join in the hunt after the enchanted boar with the razor (which was fastened to its tusk) and the comb and scissors between its ears. The lord of the castle was quite sure that King Arthur would refuse to do any such thing—but the Pig-Sty Prince knew better. Last of all his tasks was to bring Olwen's father the sword of a terrible giant. This giant could only be slain by his own sword, and would certainly kill anyone who tried to steal it from him. But the Pig-Sty Prince was not daunted even by the thought of the giant.

"My lord and kinsman, King Arthur, will obtain all these marvels for me!" he cried fearlessly. "I will have not only your daughter, O great lord with the unkempt hair, but I will have also your life!"

So saying, he departed from the castle, and all King Arthur's warriors departed with him.

They journeyed for a whole day and, in the evening, arrived at another castle, where a giant, who was as black as ebony, met them at the gate. When they asked him whose castle it was, he said that it belonged to the giant with the mighty sword, and nobody who went into it ever came out alive. In spite of that, Arthur's warriors went on and knocked at the door. The porter who sat inside called out to them that nobody could be admitted unless he could do something nobody else could do so well. Whereupon, Sir Kay, who was among the warriors, answered that he was the finest polisher of swords in the world.

The porter carried this news to the giant, who replied that his sword very badly wanted polishing, and ordered that Sir Kay should be admitted.

So Sir Kay was let into the castle, and the sword was given into his hand; and after polishing it and making it very sharp, he slipped behind the giant and cut off his head!

Then all the warriors rushed into the giant's castle and took the gold and silver that were hidden in it. With this treasure, and with the great sword, they traveled back to Arthur's court and told him the whole story. And, when Arthur heard of the other marvels that had yet to be performed, he asked which of them had better be undertaken first. In answer, the warriors told him that it would be best to find Mabon, the lost huntsman, who had been stolen from his mother when he was three days old.

Now, of course, Mabon had been stolen by the fairy-people, and only the fairy-people would be able to tell of his hiding place. Very close to the fairy-people lived the birds in the trees, and the stags on the mountains, and the salmon in the rivers. So, first of all, the warriors went in search of the talking blackbird.

They found the blackbird flying about a glen, and when they asked her where Mabon could be found, she said she would show them the way to a certain fairy stag, who might be able to help them, as he was many years older than she was. So off they all set to find the fairy stag. When they found him, they told him that they were the messengers of King Arthur, and that they were seeking Mabon, who had been stolen from his mother when he was three days old.

The stag answered that there was an owl who was much older than he was, and who might possibly be able to answer their question. As they were Arthur's messengers, he added, he would lead them to the owl. Once more, they formed a procession, with the stag and the blackbird in front, and moved on over the hills till they found the fairy owl.

But the owl could not tell them where Mabon had been hidden. All he could do was to lead them to another bird, still older than himself—the great eagle of the crags. And the eagle it was who told them of the great and wonderful fairy salmon.

The eagle had once tried to kill the salmon, but they had become friends afterwards, and so, when the mighty bird led Arthur's messengers to the mighty fish, the salmon answered that he knew where Mabon was, and he took two of the messengers upon his wide silver shoulders and swam up the river with them to the stone walls of an old city. And there they heard somebody crying and lamenting in a dungeon—and it was Mabon, who had been stolen from his mother when he was only three days old.

Then the warriors went back to Arthur's court, and the King gathered together an army and came to the old stone city and attacked the dungeon, and set Mabon free and took him home to his own castle. And then they all began to ask each other which marvel it would be best that they should next seek, now that Mabon had been set free.

This time, they thought they would seek out a certain she-wolf who had two wolf-cubs that she took out hunting with her. For the cubs were really enchanted men, and it would help everybody if they were set free. So they found the she-wolf, and Arthur set free the wolf-cubs, who would certainly, had they remained in wolf-shapes, have interfered in the chase after the great boar with the razor fastened to his tusk and the fairy comb and scissors hanging between his two ears. On the way back from this adventure with the she-wolf, one of Arthur's warriors saved a whole anthill full of ants from being burned by a great fire that was sweeping over the country. And the ants were so grateful that they burrowed into the earth and brought out every one of the nine bushels of flax seed that the Pig-Sty Prince had promised to take back to the father of Princess Olwen.

Well, things seemed to be getting on now, and the marvels were really being performed, one by one. But the fairy hound and the fairy leash and the fairy collar had still to be discovered. As Sir Kay was talking all this over with Sir Bedivere, they suddenly saw a great smoke from a great fire, and they thought it was the fire of a robber. They hurried off in the direction of the fire, and there, sure enough, was the greatest robber that Arthur had ever hunted, roasting some boar's flesh on a spit. And Sir Kay, pointing to the robber's beard, whispered to Sir Bedivere that only the living hairs from that beard could make the fairy leash that would hold the fairy hound with which Mabon must hunt the enchanted boar who carried the comb and the scissors and the razor.

So the two warriors hid themselves until the robber had eaten so much supper that he fell fast asleep. Then they stole up to him and actually managed, not only to dig a great pit under his feet while he slept, but to tip him into it without waking him up. When he was fast in the pit, they plucked out the hairs of his beard, and then killed him outright; and, as he was a very wicked robber indeed, the world was better for his death.

Carrying the leash which they had made of the robber's beard, they returned to Arthur's court. "Now," said King Arthur, "what is to be the next marvel?" And they were all agreed immediately that it was to be the capture of the fairy hound.

They had to search through many countries, but at last they found the fairy hound in the Enchanted Forest itself, and took it home to Arthur's castle. And now they were all ready to hunt the boar with the comb and the scissors and the razor. But it was such a great and terrible animal that Arthur said they would not start upon the hunt until they were quite sure it really *had* the comb and scissors hanging between its ears. So he made one of his knights take the form of a bird, and, in this form, fly to the mountain where the enchanted boar was hidden. The bird-knight flew right down onto the top of the boar's den, and, sure enough, there were the comb, and the scissors, and the razor. But when he tried to snatch them in his bird-claws, he only succeeded in getting hold of one of the boar's bristles, which made the fierce creature very angry indeed.

For a time, Arthur decided to leave the boar alone, and obtain the magic cauldron. Now the cauldron was in the house of a great king, who kept all his money in it, and entirely refused to part with it at Arthur's request. So Arthur made war on him and conquered him, and carried away the cauldron, money and all. And by this time everybody was amazed at the things that King Arthur would do rather than break his promise to the Pig-Sty Prince who wanted to marry the Princess Olwen.

And now the day had arrived for the great hunting, but all the enchanted boars of the country heard of it, and turned out, themselves, to fight the warriors of Arthur's court. Chief among these great boars was a huge beast with bristles like silver wire that made a shining pathway as he rushed through the trees. Arthur's warriors and Mabon and the fairy hound had terrible battles with the boars; but at last the great beast with the comb and the scissors and the razor was driven into the river, not far from the very city where Mabon had been found by the two knights who rode on the shoulders of the fairy salmon.

Then, while the huge creature lashed the water, Mabon himself sprang upon it and snatched the razor from its tusk and hid it under his vest. But nobody could reach the comb and the scissors, until a very brave warrior followed Mabon into the water and managed to get hold of the scissors. However, before either man could secure the comb, the boar scrambled out of the water and galloped off, never stopping for at least a hundred miles. Then King Arthur himself set off after it, with a whole host of knights, and at last they overtook it, and, after a terrific fight, got possession of the comb, while the enchanted boar was driven into the ocean and never seen again.

Then King Arthur and his warriors took a short rest, after which the King asked if there were still any more marvels to be performed. And his knights answered that the blood of the black witch had yet to be obtained. So the King set off in search of the black witch and found her hiding in a cave, and she nearly killed two of the warriors the moment they entered her hiding-place. So King Arthur instantly took his sword and leaped into the cave and cut the ugly black witch in two. And one of his attendants took the fairy blood and put it into a fairy basin, to take to the father of the Princess Olwen.

Now, as Arthur's messengers had obtained the witch's blood and the magical razor and the fairy comb and scissors, they thought that the other tasks might wait a while, and they all went back to the horrible lord's castle with their spoils. They sprinkled his hair and beard with the witch's blood, and then, in spite of his struggles, cut both of them off and shaved him as clean as an ivory ball. Then, as the loss of his hair and beard made him quite helpless, they found it easy to chop off his head with the giant's sword. After which, they took possession of the castle and all the gold and silver and jewels that were hidden in it.

As the father of the Princess was dead, there was really no need now to trouble about the other marvels that he had declared were to be performed for her wedding day. The Pig-Sty Prince therefore married her without them, and he and his bride and Arthur's knights and warriors made festival for at least a week in the castle. And for hundreds of years afterwards all the old folk of the countryside would tell of the marvels which were performed at the command of King Arthur in order that the Pig-Sty Prince might marry the Princess Olwen.

Nobody rejoiced more at the performance of the marvels and the success of the Pig-Sty Prince than did the blackbird and the stag, the

Pig-Sty Prince and the Many Travels

owl, the eagle and the salmon, all of whom had helped Arthur's knights to discover the place where Mabon was kept in prison. These fairy animals, as you know, were very, very old—so old that they could hardly remember the time when they were young, and they had lived among the mountains and valleys for hundreds of years. The blackbird judged of time by a smith's anvil, near which she always built her nest. No smith had worked at the anvil since she came there, but every evening she had sharpened her beak upon it, and by the time Arthur's messengers came, the anvil had been worn down to the size of a nut. As for the stag, he had sheltered each night under an oak sapling and had watched it grow into a great oak with a hundred branches, and then wither away and die. But the owl, who was much, much older, had come when the whole valley was a wooded glen, and had seen a race of men root up the trees and plant others, and their remote descendants, and again theirs, do the same, so that the wood in which the owl now sheltered was the fourth wood. As for the eagle, he had sat for hundreds of years upon a crag, once so high that he could peck at the stars, and now but a yard above the ground. While the salmon had been speared with fifty spears, which he carried about in his silver back until the eagle pulled them out for him. Everybody in those days knew the stories of the owl and the blackbird, the stag, the eagle, and the salmon, for these fairy animals had relations who lived in the Enchanted Forest, and the stag was first cousin to the white stag of the fairy-hunt. There is little doubt that Merlin had ridden upon his back of a moonlit night, followed by the beautiful hinds and fawns. As for the salmon, he was the most wonderful of all these old, old creatures, and the reason why he had so many spears in his back was because many hunters had sought for him in the rocky pools, and thrust their long spears into him to try to bring him to land. But he had always broken away, for he was the greatest fairy salmon living and knew most of the secrets of the world. The fishes caught by the Rich Fisher were the children, and grandchildren, and great-grandchildren of this salmon, and King Arthur knew very well what a wonderful thing it was that such a mighty and mysterious fish should have given his help toward enabling the Pig-Sty Prince to marry the Princess Olwen.

The Knight of the Sparrow-Hawk

King Arthur held his court not only at beautiful Camelot, but also at a place called Caerlon. The castle there had seven doors, with a magnificent porter seated at each one, to open and shut it when the knights and ladies passed. These porters were very clever, as they had to bar the way to enemies as well as to make it free for friends. At night they went to bed, all except one, who marched round the castle from door to door. This one had cat's eyes, large and green and pale, so that he could see in the darkness just as well as in the light.

Well, one' evening a handsome, unknown youth, dressed in yellow satin, came running up to the porter with the cat's eyes and told him that there was a mysterious white stag in the wood over the river. The porter hurried to tell Arthur; for, ever since the Fairy Hunt of which you have read, the King had vowed there should never be a white stag near his castle that he would not follow. So, as soon as the dawn broke next morning, the whole court set off a-hunting—horns blowing, hounds baying, and horses prancing, as excited as you please. The white stag meant a fairy adventure for one of the knights, of that everybody was certain. They wondered which knight had been marked today to travel deep into the Enchanted Forest and to bring back a fresh secret from Fairyland.

Now, Queen Guinevere was late that morning, and the hunt was almost out of sight when she came tripping down the stone stairs into the castle hall. She asked where Arthur had gone, and was told by her ladies that he had ridden off to hunt a great white stag in the ferny woods. Guinevere pouted for a minute; then, all at once, she clapped her hands joyfully and declared that she would go a-hunting after the King! So she and her maidens dressed themselves very quickly, and set off on horseback, their pretty veils waving and their faces as bright and mischievous as the faces of children.

As they rode through the trees, they heard a great galloping behind them, and up came one of the very handsomest knights of the Round Table. He had long golden hair, and a long golden sword, and a blue-purple scarf round his shoulders, with a golden apple at every corner. His legs were bare, the better to grip the sides of his horse, which was very strong and tall, and had a long black mane, and a tail that was even blacker and longer.

"It is good young Geraint!" cried the ladies

The Knight of the Sparrow-Hawk   155

when they saw him. "Oh, handsome and brave Geraint, are you coming with us and with the Queen?"

Now, Geraint had really intended to gallop after Arthur as fast as he could, for he, too, was late this morning. But when the ladies asked him if he were going to escort the Queen, he could not possibly say he was not. So he bowed very low, drew in his prancing horse, and joined the pretty company of maidens, giving up all idea of the adventure for which he had been hoping he was the chosen knight of the day.

But no sooner had he drawn near the side of the Queen, than the adventure, which he thought he had given up, came riding through the wood toward him, in the shape of an enormous knight with his face quite hidden under his helmet. On one side of this giant stranger rode a lady dressed in royally rich brocade; on the other pranced a hideous little dwarf. As they trotted abreast through the wood, Guinevere pulled up her horse and stared at them in amazement. Then the newcomers also drew rein, and, standing still at a little distance, seemed to talk among themselves.

The Queen, frankly curious, shook her horse's bridle and trotted off across the turf to speak to them. The dwarf was the nearest to her, and, pausing as she came up to him, she asked him the name of the big knight with the hidden face. But the dwarf, who was the ugliest little man you ever saw in your life, answered by striking the Queen with a long wand that he carried in his hand.

Then such a shout as you never heard before rang through the wood from Geraint! All the ladies, too, cried out in anger. Before anybody could do anything, however, off galloped the strange knight, still with the lady and the dwarf on either hand. And off after them tore young Geraint, calling, at the top of his voice, that he would avenge the Queen!

Such a chase the three led him, right through the wood, and over the mountain, and down into a valley where you could see the towers and roofs of a great city. Through the gates they rode, with Geraint still hard on their heels. He saw that all the people stood still and saluted the knight and the lady as they galloped past; and he noticed, even in his haste, that the courtyards of the houses were full of men, who were polishing shields, and burnishing swords, and washing armor, and shoeing horses. Then the knight and the dwarf and the lady galloped up a hill to a great castle. Its gates were immediately opened with sounds of welcome. The three rode in, and the entrance was closed and barred behind them.

As Geraint pulled up his horse, weary and bitterly disappointed, he saw that he was close to a ruined palace, which could be approached by way of an old marble bridge that spanned a deep river. He crossed the bridge and was met on the

The Knight of the Sparrow-Hawk

other side by an old man who wore very ragged clothing, but whose voice was gentle and his manner gracious. This old man invited the knight into the ruined palace, where he was met by an old woman, also in rags, but sweet and dignified. With her was her daughter, whose face and hair were beautiful above her poor, rough clothing. They, too, greeted Geraint in soft voices, and offered him what they could in the way of meat and drink.

As he ate, the beautiful girl, who was named Enid, looked after his horse, and he watched her with deep admiration in his eyes. Then the poor old couple told him that they were the real lord and lady of the city, but had been turned out of their home by the Knight of the Sparrow-Hawk. He was the knight whom Geraint had been following, and he lived now in the castle, and every year he held a tournament in the meadow just below it. In this meadow a Sparrow-Hawk, set up between two high three-pronged spears, was always the prize of the day. Whoever won it was called "Knight of the Sparrow-Hawk" for a whole year, with the right to live in the castle, and to rule over the land. But as the knight himself always won, by fair means or foul, there was not really much use in anybody else entering the tournament and doing battle for the prize.

Geraint listened, and his heart beat high with hope. "*I* will fight for the Sparrow-Hawk tomorrow," he cried. "I will conquer the knight whose dwarf insulted Queen Guinevere, and I will force him to return your castle and your riches to you, from whom he stole them."

The poor old couple looked at him, then at each other, and shook their heads.

"No knight can fight for the Sparrow-Hawk unless the lady is with him whom he thinks the fairest lady in the world. Long ago, this magic was made in the meadow. It is because the Knight of the Sparrow-Hawk never stirs without his lady that he is always able to win the prize."

"His lady may be beautiful, but she is not half so beautiful as your daughter yonder!" cried Geraint eagerly. "Never have I seen a maiden as fair as she."

The words were no sooner out of his mouth than the old couple rose to their feet in great excitement.

"If you indeed believe that," said they, "if you do really and truly believe it, then take our daughter with you into the meadow tomorrow! We will find some armor for you, and she will make it possible for you to win, because of the magic of which we have told you."

The next morning dawned beautiful and clear, and a great gathering came together, very early indeed, in the meadow where the Sparrow-Hawk was set up between the two three-pronged spears. When everybody had arrived, a great blast of

The Knight of the Sparrow-Hawk

trumpets was blown at the castle gates, they were flung open, and out rode the enormous knight, with, as usual, the dwarf upon his right hand and the lady upon his left. He drew rein, and his heralds cried out the proclamation. Was there anyone present who would come forward and fight for the Sparrow-Hawk that was set up between the two three-pronged spears?

Nobody stirred, and the great knight turned to his lady and bade her go, take the Sparrow-Hawk upon her hand, and bring it to him. But just as she was about to set off, a young knight in old, rusty armor, on a very tired, half-lame horse, rode forward; and at his side a maiden in rags walked quietly, with neither shoes nor stockings upon her little white feet, and only a coarse hood upon her head.

"My lady is fairer than yours!" shouted young Geraint. "Come! I will fight you for the Sparrow-Hawk, and call down the magic of the meadow to help me! Victory will be mine, for the sweet maiden, Enid, is the loveliest and noblest lady in all the land."

Then the two knights rushed upon each other with a great crash of arms, while the lady in the royal brocade and the lady in rags looked on. Everybody had burst out laughing at Geraint—at his lame horse and his rusty armor, and at the beggar-maid he declared was the fairest lady in all the land. But soon their laughter changed to amazement and admiration, for, with right goodwill, the young stranger hacked, and struck, and dodged his enemy, until he proved himself by far the cleverer and stronger. And at last a great ringing shout went up from the whole multitude of watchers, for they saw the great knight of the castle thrown to the ground, where he lay, stunned and motionless, while Geraint rode up to the Sparrow-Hawk, took it upon his wrist, and, carrying it to a very old man and a very old woman among the crowd, presented it to them with the grace of a prince making an offering to his lawful king and queen.

Then another shout went up from the people! They recognized in the poor beggars their rightful lady and their rightful lord. Leaving Geraint to look after the fallen knight, they escorted the old man and woman back into the castle that had been stolen from them. There Geraint presently followed, with beautiful Enid, and with the great defeated knight bound in chains. As for the lady and the dwarf, they had already fled. But all the people were shouting with excitement and gladness; for, indeed, they were delighted to see their true lord and lady restored to their own home.

Then sweet Enid went upstairs to her own dainty chamber, where she had lived as a little girl, and dressed herself in soft silks, and a gossamer veil, and long chains of shining gems. She came down, looking like a princess, and Geraint

fell more deeply in love with her than ever. But he asked her to put on her old frock again, in which, he said, he would take her to Arthur's court, and there they would be married. Also, he explained, he could not marry his fair lady until the insult to Queen Guinevere had been wiped out. The Knight of the Sparrow-Hawk must ride after them to Arthur's court, and must, in his own person, apologize fully and humbly for the behavior of his dwarf!

So they set off: Geraint and his lady, and the knight in chains behind.

When they reached Caerleon, Geraint led both his bride and his prisoner into the presence of the Queen. The big knight apologized as humbly as anyone could wish, and was sent away again. But Geraint married Enid, with everyone's full approval, and the Queen herself gave the wedding dress, and the happy pair remained at the court of King Arthur for the rest of their lives.

The Little Prince of the Lake

After the day when King Arthur and King Pellinore and Sir Gawaine had followed the elfin hunt into the heart of Fairyland, most wonderful adventures began to happen, not only to them, but to all the other knights of the Round Table. You shall hear of these adventures one by one. To brave the mysterious dangers of the Enchanted Forest, and the Castle Perilous, and the Valley of No Return was the greatest sign of courage that anyone could show. So, of course, when the King came back again (for he came back, safe enough) and told of the things that he had seen and heard, every one of his followers wanted to go into Fairyland and see these marvels for themselves. One by one, they went; and, on their return, told the story of their adventures, which indeed were as thrilling as anyone could wish. The fame of Arthur's fearless knights was soon spread far and wide. Every brave and romantic youth wanted to come and make his vow of fealty to the great King who was the head of such a gallant company. And among these youths was a Prince called Lancelot, who had spent all his childhood in

Fairyland, in a way that you shall read about in the following story.

He was the son of a great King named Ban, whose castle was built in a valley between two mountain ranges. When Lancelot was only a little baby, a neighboring King, called Claudas, came riding one day over the eastern range with an enormous army behind him. This great, glittering army set up its tents all round King Ban's castle, and prepared to besiege it. For a long time, King Ban and his soldiers held out against King Claudas and the big army, but at last they were obliged to give in. Their food and water were finished, and the soldiers could not get past the tents of the enemy to bring back to the castle the meat and bread and wine that were so badly needed.

So then King Ban sent a messenger to King Claudas, asking leave for himself and the Queen and their little son to leave their home and to go and place themselves under the protection of the great King Arthur. Claudas consented, but only on condition that the castle was handed over to him immediately. So poor King Ban handed over his castle, and set off very, very sorrowfully on a big horse, with the weeping Queen in the saddle behind him. On a second horse rode just one faithful servant, carrying the baby prince, Lancelot.

They rode a little way down the valley, and then King Ban said he could not bear to leave

his beautiful castle without one look at it from the top of the nearest hill. So the Queen took the baby into her arms and sat down by the side of a beautiful clear lake, while the King and the faithful servant rode together to the top of the mountain.

For a long time, after the sound of their horses' hoofs had passed away, everything was very quiet in the valley. You could hear nothing but little birds singing, and sometimes the rustle of the wind in the treetops or of the water fowl among the reeds. The Queen, who had dried her tears, played almost contentedly with the baby, consoled by its beauty and its merriment. By and by, however, she became anxious, for she thought that the King had been away a very long time. The baby was asleep by now, so she laid it down among the meadow flowers, covered it with her cloak, and set off on foot up the rocky path that led to the top of the hill.

She had not gone more than a hundred yards or so when she heard a queer, chuckling laugh behind her—just like the chuckle of a water hen among the rushes, only much longer and more mischievous. She turned round, very quickly, to see who was laughing. And what do you think she saw?

She saw her little baby, the most precious thing she had, ten thousand times more precious than the castle, in the arms of a strange and beautiful lady. This lady's gown rippled about her like water in the moonlight; her long golden hair was wreathed with forget-me-nots and silver shells; her white arms shone like alabaster; and she wore a necklace and bracelets of the most lovely precious stones in the world.

She had taken the baby onto a big gray rock, that jutted out from the land toward the center of the lake. She was rocking it in her arms and laughing. At the moment the Queen caught sight of her, she began to sing.

The words seemed to be a fairy lullaby, but the poor Queen did not pause to listen. With a loud cry, she set off, running, to rescue her little baby. But the fairy saw her coming. She sprang up on the rock, joined her two pretty white feet together, and, with the baby still in her arms, dived, like a silvery, shining arrow, straight into the green waters of the lake. A sound like a clap of thunder echoed all down the valley, and a sudden wind lashed the water into white foam. The lightning played among the trees, like the flames of a witch's fire, and long, loud peals of laughter mingled with the terrible storm. It lasted just for a minute, then went as suddenly as it had come. Everything was still again; the lake glimmered green and calm. But the fairy lady and the baby Prince had disappeared, not leaving a single sign of their existence behind them.

The poor, distracted Queen ran up and down

the banks of the lake, wringing her hands and calling out her baby's name. As she wept and called, the faithful servant came hurrying down the side of the mountain. He, too, was sobbing. He said that wicked King Claudas had set fire to the castle, which was blazing away into ruins; and that King Ban was lying at the top of the hill, dead with grief.

Then the Queen dried her eyes, and folded her hands, and spoke calmly:

"My husband has gone. My baby has gone. My home has gone," she said. "There is nothing left for me to live for. I may as well die, too."

But even as she said this, the Abbess of a convent not far away came walking, wrapped in her cloak, along the banks of the lake. She was a good and sweet woman, and she knew all about the fairy in the silver robes, with white hands and golden hair, who lived under the water. She heard the Queen's sad words, and, coming up to her, she spoke consolingly.

"Poor Queen!" she said—"for, indeed, I know you are a Queen—be comforted! You have not lost as much as you think you have. Your little baby is in hands far safer than those of any human nurse! For your husband, the King, be content. He is at peace. For yourself, there is a home waiting in the convent there, among the trees. Dry your tears and come with me."

The Abbess spoke so gently, and yet so firmly, that somehow an extraordinary feeling of consolation came over the poor Queen. She went to the convent with this good woman, and found it was a beautiful and restful place. The Abbess kept telling her that the baby was, indeed, in the very best of hands. So by and by, the Queen, who was tired of wars and troubles, settled down in contentment, and stayed with the good Abbess in the peaceful convent until she died.

But what had happened to the baby?

Well, the beautiful fairy dived down, down, down, carrying little Lancelot in her arms. As she dived, her silver gown mingled with the silver ripples, and the shells and forget-me-nots floated away from her golden hair. Then, far below her, appeared the roofs and towers of an enchanted city. And now the water turned into a cloudy mist, and her robes spread out into two glittering wings. She was no longer diving, but floating on the misty air. Softly, very softly, she floated downward, till the bright streets, and flowery gardens, and marble walls of the enchanted city showed quite clearly beneath. Then she stretched out her little white feet and alighted on the very tips of her toes, all among the tall green grass and fairy buttercups and daisies. And from every side beautiful ladies came running up to her, exclaiming and shouting and clapping their hands. They were, every one of them, fairies of the lake, and they were so pleased to have got a little human baby that they did not know what to do.

Tiny Lancelot had been sleeping all this time, and, because he was in the arms of a water-fairy, he had been able to breathe quite comfortably all the way down through the lake. Now he woke up, and smiled at the pretty ladies clustering round him.

When he smiled they all cried out, with greater delight than ever, that his eyes were just like their own forget-me-nots. They kissed him, and hugged him, and took off his little Prince's clothes, and dressed him up in silvery gossamers, just as they were dressed themselves.

Then they took him into one of the enchanted houses and gave him a wonderful nursery all to himself, where he had fishes to play with him all day long. And he was so merry and healthy that they called him the "beautiful foundling," or, sometimes, "the happy child."

But the fairy-lady who had brought him there, and who was the Queen of them all, never called him by either of these names. She had but one title for him that she used always, and her voice was very gentle when she spoke it.

This title was "Son of a King." Because, you see, she knew that he was of royal human blood, and that, someday, he must go back to the world, from Fairyland, and play his part, as a Prince, among his fellow-men.

And how Lancelot of the Lake went back to the world from the enchanted city under the water you shall hear in another story.

The Wizard Bewitched

Merlin was growing very old now, and his work at Arthur's court was nearly finished. He had made the Round Table for the knights who took the great Vow; and he had set the Seat Perilous at the King's right hand. No knight had as yet ventured to take his place on that mysterious seat. If ever one or another approached it, the fiery letters would suddenly shine out in golden flame: "This is the Seat Perilous." And the murmur would, once more, pass from mouth to mouth of those who sat at the Round Table: "That is the Seat Perilous! No knight must sit in it today, nor tomorrow, nor for many years to come!"

The great magician no longer rode on his fairy stag over the hills at nighttime, nor took on the disguise of a bright-haired, laughing youth. He let his beard grow very long and white, and he would sit outside the great doors of Camelot, singing to himself and playing on a harp that he held in his long magician's fingers. And with him, very often, in those days, would sit the fairy Nimue, who was, as you know, one of the Ladies of the Lake.

She had changed her name to Vivian; for Nimue was too strange a title for any human lady to bear. Since King Pellinore had brought her back to Arthur's court, she had behaved as much like a flesh-and-blood princess as she could manage. But she was never anything, really, but one of the Ladies of the Lake—a mysterious elfin thing, with mermaid's eyes that were green and dark, like the shadows you may see in mountain tarns. She knew a lot of magic herself, and in the old days had often peeped in at Merlin as he sat in his house with the seventy windows and the sixty doors. It had been in obedience to the old wizard's orders that she had helped to make the wonderful and high adventure of the Fairy Hunt, which had carried off King Arthur into the Enchanted Forest so soon after his wedding day. And now, it seemed to her, the old magician was growing weary of the world, and she thought that it would be rather nice for him to go away and live happily forever in Fairyland.

Often she would persuade him to sing to her, and, also, to tell her stories of the magic that he had made in his life. Her eyes would grow dark and bright with excitement as she listened, and she would twist her golden hair round her white fingers, and tap her little feet on the grass. Then she would ask him to walk with her in the woods and meadows, and she would make wreaths of wild roses and lilies, and hang them on her pretty neck and arms as they talked. Or she would lead him to the ferny brink of a deep pool and ask him if it were not like the fountain in Broceliande, over which the tall green tree bent its branches, and where the little birds sang so sweetly after rain. And when night fell, she would persuade him to wander farther and farther into the forest, and to talk to her of the fiery dragon that had once lain coiled up among the stars. More particularly, she would speak of the seven rays that shone over the west—for, said she, she thought those seven rays were seven fairies, of which she, herself, was one.

Then she would try to make him speak of the Silver Table, and the Rich Fisher, and the Shining Cup; and ask him where he had hidden the little book in which it was all written down. But this Merlin would never tell her. It had nothing, so he said, to do with any lady, let alone a Lady of the Lake. For he knew well enough that she was only a fairy from Fairyland. Yet she fascinated him more and more! Because, you see, he kept telling her secret after secret, so that she was spinning webs of his own magic about him all the time.

One night they had been wandering in the woods together, as usual, and Merlin, cold and weary, was walking slowly home alone. Vivian still lingered by the side of a lake in which were bright reflections of the stars. She loved the cool water, with its deep, still shadows, better than any human home. But Merlin still turned wistfully back to Camelot after his long days with the fairy in the forest. Tonight he was thinking deeply of Arthur and all the other knights of the Round Table. Above all, he was wondering when that knight would come who could sit safely in the Perilous Seat. Because Merlin knew that this knight, and he only, would be the knight who would be able to go into that far, mysterious place where Joseph had hidden the Silver Table and the Holy Grail.

As he thought about these things, all at once a voice came through the trees, and he saw an old, old man leaning upon his staff, who spoke his name, "Merlin."

"Who are you?" said Merlin, startled.

"I am Blaise, the hermit who christened you many, many years ago. Merlin, I have come to warn you. Your own enchantments are being woven round you! If you go on teaching your Lady of the Lake any more secrets, she will cast a spell on you that even you will not be able to break, and she will keep you in Fairyland forever."

Merlin sighed. He tried to see Blaise's face through the shadows, but it was very dark.

"Good Blaise," said he, "what am I but half a fairy, myself! I have done, I think, all that I was meant to do. I have set King Arthur on the throne of his father; I have made the Round Table; I have explained the letters written in the Seat Perilous. The Shining Cup is still hidden, but I do not think I am meant to wait at Arthur's court until it is found. I would be glad to go into some far country —say, to Broceliande—and to rest there in the green forests forever."

Blaise waited a minute or two, then spoke again.

"It may be as you say," he answered. "Perhaps your work is really done. It has been a good work, Merlin. The wicked mountain demons have lost much of their power since the Round Table was made. They will lose it all when once the Shining Cup has been found again. And for the Ladies of the Lake—well, they are kindly and helpful to men. Did they not give the King his sword Excalibur? So go your way, Merlin! Rest, if you like, forever by the side of the woodland fountain, under the branches of the tall green tree!"

The hermit's voice died away; and even while Merlin looked, Blaise seemed to be swallowed up in the shadows of the wood. But slipping starrily through the trees, he saw the bright nymph, Vivian, coming to him again.

"Great wizard," she said, putting her little, cool hand in his. "Come! Come away with me to Brittany! Come to Broceliande!"

Merlin laid his arm round her shoulders. "If I should go with you to Broceliande," he said, "I do not think that I should ever come back again!"

"Never mind, never mind!" whispered the fairy. "Only come!"

She drew him across the dim, dewy meadows until they reached the seashore. There, under the stars, a little boat was rocking—one of the fairy boats that belonged to the Ladies of the Lake.

"Come!" whispered Vivian once more. And this time, Merlin gave way without another word.

So they sailed away to Brittany, and to Broceliande, where the green tree grew over the magical fountain that Gawaine, and only Gawaine, had found. But the Lady of the Lake knew every inch of the ferny path that led to it. As she drew Merlin toward it, she gathered the fern seeds and tossed them about him.

"It is the Eve of St. John," said she. "The fern seeds would make even a human being invisible! What will they do to *you*, do you think?"

But Merlin only smiled at her in the moonlight, without answering. And they went on, side by side.

Then, before them, they saw whitethorn bushes glimmering pale, and, above the bushes, the tall green tree. They reached the fairy fountain, and sat down beside it.

"See!" said Vivian. "Here is the white marble slab, and the silver bowl fastened with the silver chain! But no knight is guarding the fairy well tonight!"

The Wizard Bewitched

"Why should it be guarded?" asked Merlin, laying his hand on the marble. "The fountain is mine—has always been mine! The secrets of its waters are mine. This white stone is mine. See! My name is written there!"

Vivian looked, and sure enough, she saw letters of gold appear, just for a moment, on the marble slab:

"I am the Stone of Merlin."

They shone there, exactly like the letters on the Seat Perilous, and then they faded away. The fairy drew nearer to the wizard, and he laid one hand on her hair, while, with the other, he fingered the silver bowl.

"Are all the secrets of Fairyland yours, Merlin?"

"Most of them, sweet Lady of the Lake. Most of them! They are strange secrets, but the greatest of all lies under that stone!"

"What is it? Tell me! What is it?"

"It is the secret of Sleep," said Merlin dreamily. "Of Sleep that can make a man lie and dream from day to day, from month to month, from year to year. I could almost wish I were folded in such a strange, sweet Sleep."

"Tell me!" said the fairy again. "Tell me!"

She was eager to know, half from curiosity, half from the desire for power. And so Merlin told her, at last, the song and the dance that would draw from that mysterious stone its great secret of unending Sleep.

Then the fairy stood up, and while he watched her, still dreamily, she began to sing, very softly, and to weave a fairy ring all about the tired old wizard, and the white marble slab, and the magic pool. And, as she sang and danced, Merlin's weary eyes closed, and his head drooped low on his chest, down which streamed his long white beard. Then a little silver mist, like pearly air, crept up from the fountain and out from underneath the fairy stone. And the magician's head bent lower and lower, until at last he lay beside the mysterious fountain in Broceliande, fast asleep.

Vivian stopped singing and dancing, and stood looking at him in the moonlight, her eyes more like green water than ever. The leaf-shadows flickered over her, and over the sleeping wizard, and the pearly mist grew thicker. At last, the dew from it seemed to drip all over the fairy's hair; and she laughed, for it reminded her of her own lovely lake. So gathering her gleaming robes round her, she slid away like a silver shadow, back to her own enchanted waters, leaving Merlin sleeping soundly and calmly, in the fairy mist, under the tall green tree.

The Adventure of Sir Bors

Sir Bors was a very big knight, tall and strong, as you might have guessed from the sound of his name. One day he was riding along a grassy road when he saw a building with high gray walls and towers like a castle, half-hidden among great clumps of fine trees. A river ran around it; and across the river was arched a stone bridge.

The look of the castle attracted Sir Bors very much. He turned his horse's head that way and, trotting over the bridge, drew near to the handsome building. A knight rode out through the gates and tried to stop his way. But Sir Bors fought with him and conquered him. Then, sparing the other's life, he rode proudly into the courtyard of the castle, and was met by the King who owned it.

The King's name was Pelles, and he was always ready to welcome a brave and merciful knight. He greeted Sir Bors courteously, and led him into the great hall. And no sooner was Sir Bors inside than he felt a strange awe and wonder creeping over him. It seemed to him that this castle was not like any other castle in the world.

It was full of such strange lights and shadows, such whisperings and rustlings, such coolness and perfume. Little birds, like jewels, flew about the gold and purple glass of the windows. Their wings were almost transparent, their heads bore tiny crowns. And prettiest of all among them was a white one, like a tiny dove, that flitted again and again through the shadowy hall, carrying in her bill a little golden goblet hung on three chains.

"Truly," thought Sir Bors to himself, "I am in the very heart of Fairyland!" And, indeed, if he were not, he was certainly in some place that was very much like it.

Then, while the dove still flitted about the hall, a table mysteriously appeared, covered with honeyed cakes, and ripe fruits, and crystal goblets filled with crimson wine. The knight and the King sat down to eat and drink. When they had finished, Sir Bors felt so light in body, so refreshed, so calm and rested, that he wondered what sort of fairy food he had been eating. As he wondered, he looked up and saw King Pelles watching him.

"Sir Bors," said the King gently and gravely, "you have always been a good and a pure knight."

"I hope so," answered Sir Bors. "I have wished to be."

"You must have been," replied the King, "or you would never have seen the little white dove, and eaten the mysterious food on the mysterious

table. And now something still more wonderful is going to be shown to you."

As the King finished speaking, the hall grew darker and, at the far end, a golden light appeared. Then, in the heart of the golden light, which floated all around her like a sunset cloud, appeared a slim and beautiful lady who, Sir Bors thought, looked like a fair Princess. But, when he looked again, he saw she was not flesh and blood at all. She seemed a sort of delicate spirit, and she moved like a spirit through the dim shadows of the hall, her feet barely touching the floor, her hair shining like sunlight, pale wings folded upon her shoulders, and pale hands clasped around what looked like a wondrously beautiful Silver Cup. From the mouth of the cup rose a still flame like the flame of a candle; and it was as if this flame shed all the brightness which surrounded the maiden's form.

She passed slowly by, and Sir Bors watched, breathless. Then he turned to King Pelles.

"Who is she?" he asked under his breath. "What is the Cup that she carries?"

The King answered in a voice that seemed to come from very far away:

"She is—who she is! And of the Cup you have often heard."

"Is it," whispered Sir Bors, "can it be the Cup of the spirit-world—the silver chalice that we knights call the Holy Grail?"

The Adventure of Sir Bors

"Yes," replied King Pelles. "It is the Holy Grail. Here, in this castle, it has been hidden for years. But look again!"

Then Sir Bors looked again, and down the hall, in the very track of the golden maiden, stepping through the lingering, fading radiance she had left, came a Princess with a tiny sleeping baby in her arms. She stepped softly toward Sir Bors and held the baby toward him, for him to look at. He thought he had never seen a lady so lovely, nor a child so like a flower.

"This is my daughter, the Princess Elaine," said the King, speaking more softly than ever. "And the little child is her son, Galahad. He has been born in the Castle of the Hidden Grail. He it will be who will sit in the Seat Perilous one day, on the right hand of King Arthur, the seat that has been empty so long. But when Galahad takes his seat there—"

"What?" asked Sir Bors, touching the child very gently with his big forefinger. "What?"

But King Pelles did not answer. He shook his head and fell silent again. The Princess Elaine smiled down at her little baby, and then up at Sir Bors.

"It will be a wonderful day," she said, below her breath. "The most wonderful day that the knights of the Round Table have ever seen."

"We have had many adventures," replied Sir Bors. "We have seen the Fairy Hunt and followed the great white stag! We have done homage to the Ladies of the Lake, and have slain giants, and killed terrible beasts, and taken over the guardianship of the fairy fountain under the green tree. We have wandered in the Enchanted Forest and seen the fairy salmon and ridden on his back. What is this adventure that will come with Galahad—the little baby here who is to grow up into such a wonderful knight?"

But still neither the King nor the Princess would answer. They only smiled and shook their heads, and told him to follow them up the stairs of the castle and they would show him a sight even more wonderful than all the rest.

So up the stairs of the castle went Sir Bors with the King and the Princess—who still carried the baby—leading the way. And as they went, the whisperings and the rustlings began again all around them, the little birds flew with them, the staircase windows dropped purple and silver lights upon their heads. On the Princess's shoulder alighted the small white dove, and stooped, murmuring and cooing, toward the baby, drooping the little golden bowl on the three slim chains toward the child's fingers. And tiny Galahad woke up and caught at the pretty shining thing, and cried out delightedly. While, just ahead of the procession, it seemed to Sir Bors that the spirit of the strange castle, or whoever that lovely lady might be, moved dimly yet brightly, with the Silver Cup held in her white fingers and the golden light that came from the candle-flame shining on her face and hands and hair.

They went on—up and up and up. Then, just under the high roof of the castle, they came to a closed door all studded with strong iron nails. The maiden vanished, and Sir Bors thought she had slipped through the door just as a moonbeam might slip through the glass of a window. But the King brought out a great gold key from his pocket and put it into the lock. He turned it with a grating sound and pushed the door wide open.

Then, though all was dark on the staircase, a great light, like the light of a summer day, poured out of the room under the castle roof. The little birds flew in as if they had found their home, and the white dove spread its wings, as it perched on the Princess's shoulder, and followed the rest. They all started singing with a sound as if they had settled among the blossoming branches of trees; and the scent of flowers—Sir Bors thought it was like almond bloom—came out of the room together with their music. But when he peeped in, expecting somehow to see a garden, he saw—what do you think?

Why, just a room full of shadows; and, in the midst of the room, a table exactly like the Round Table in every way, except that, instead of being made of oak, it was made of the brightest, purest silver. And in the center stood Joseph's lost Shining Cup!

Sir Bors stood and drank in the beautiful sight, with his soul gazing out of his eyes. Then, because he could stand it no longer—for he seemed to be in the heart of some place that was far more beautiful than Fairyland—he hid his face in his hands. When he uncovered his eyes again, King Pelles had closed the door and Princess Elaine was singing the baby to sleep on the stairs.

"Go back to King Arthur," said the King. "Tell him what you have seen, and bid all the knights of the Round Table wait for the coming of Galahad."

King Arthur
in the Castle Perilous

After King Arthur, and King Pellinore, and Sir Gawaine had followed the mysterious hunt into the Enchanted Forest, they never knew at what hour of the day—or of the night, either—they might not hear the horns of Fairyland blowing, and catch a glimpse of the long string of black hounds streaming through the meadow grasses after the beautiful white stag with the silver hoofs and the horns that were like the branches of trees. Many and wonderful were the adventures that befell them—and not only them, but all the other knights of the Round Table. Sometimes the Fairy Hunt led them into startling danger, sometimes into strange and beautiful places, but always they found that there was a lady in distress to be rescued, a giant to be killed, a brave gentleman to be helped, or something else to be done that was included in the great Vow.

Well, one day Arthur was hunting with his knights on the borders of the Enchanted Forest, following a big stag, which was not, however, the one with the fairy hoofs that shone so brightly upon the moss. The King rode his horse far from his companions, and presently overtook the fine stag and shot it with a strong arrow from his bow. The stag fell by the side of a river, and Arthur dismounted to see if it were quite dead. As he stood there, the dim, thrilling notes of the elfin horns came to him, and all at once, on the opposite side of the water, he caught a glimpse of the flying white deer of Fairyland, and of the shadowy, speeding bodies of the coal-black hounds.

Arthur's horse began to tremble. In another moment, it had broken free and was galloping home as fast as it could. It might well be frightened, for, as the Fairy Hunt disappeared into the shadows of the forest, the whole wood went suddenly quite dark, while down the glimmering black waters of the river a little ship came sailing, with a hundred torches burning in a hundred silver holders, and lighting it from end to end. Nobody was steering or guiding the ship, but it sailed on as if a clever hand were at the helm; and when it reached the place where Arthur stood, it swung about on the water and lay rocking, as if it were at anchor, close against the bank where the willows grew.

"Now here is my adventure!" said King Arthur to himself, quite joyful and fearless. "It is plain that this little ship lit up with a hundred torches has come to take me somewhere."

In his green hunting-dress, he strode down through the willows and boarded the ship. Off it floated again, the moment he was aboard. And when he looked up at the sails above his head, he saw that they were all made of white silk, embroidered with pink roses and poppies the color of blood.

The little ship went on down the river, and the flaming torches were mirrored in the dark stream like so many stars. The King seemed to be quite alone on board, when, all at once, rising up, as it seemed, from the water, twelve beautiful maidens appeared and made a ring around about him, joining hands and dancing as prettily as fairies do dance, on a moonlit night, around anybody who is lucky enough to be able to see them. Then they all fell on their knees and said how glad they were that he had boarded the little ship, and what a beautiful feast was spread for him, if he would go below. So below King Arthur went, and found a cabin hung with white satin, and silver candlesticks, with clear-burning candles set on a table spread with fruit and honey, white bread, and red wine. He sat down to eat, and the twelve beautiful maidens waited on him. When he had finished they led him to a bedroom hung with crimson satin, and he lay down on a blue and silver bed and fell asleep.

But when he awoke, the pretty ship and the blue and silver bed and the crimson satin of the hangings had all disappeared! He found himself in a dark dungeon, lying on a stone floor, with twenty other knights, who were all groaning in the deepest trouble and asking one another if nobody would ever come to help them.

King Arthur sat up and rubbed his eyes. "Where am I?" he asked the knights. "And who are all of you?"

"Alas! Alas!" cried all the twenty at once. "We are twenty prisoners, and we have been thrown into this dungeon by the cruel lord of the castle. And here he will keep us until we die of hunger, as many have died here before us. For we can only be rescued when a knight has been found who is brave enough and strong enough to fight with the lord of the castle and to conquer him. And that nobody is ever likely to do."

"But, indeed, there is now a knight among you who is quite brave enough and strong enough to try!" cried King Arthur. "Here is the adventure to which I have been brought by a little ship with silken sails and twelve dancing fairies aboard. Tell me how to get out of this dungeon, and I will soon challenge the lord of the castle to fight!"

Even as he said the words, a light seemed to appear from nowhere, and he saw a beautiful girl dressed like a Princess standing beside him with a lamp in her hand.

"Follow me!" said the maiden. "I am the Princess of this castle. And I want these poor prisoners saved."

Immediately, King Arthur sprang to his feet and followed her.

She led him out of the dungeon, and all the twenty knights rose to their feet and followed as soon as the fair lady had unlocked and opened the door. She took them all to the hall of the castle and gave King Arthur armor to wear over his green hunting clothes. And she pointed to a war-horse that stood, champing its bit, in the courtyard outside.

"Mount the horse!" said she. "Take your sword, your shield, and your spear! The lord of the castle is in the meadow on his great black steed, waiting for someone to do battle with him for his prisoners. Every morning he waits, trotting up and down. But nobody ever comes. They know too well how very small is the chance they have against him!"

Arthur was already dressed in the bright armor, and he had taken up his shield and spear. But when he looked at the sword, he shook his head.

"I cannot fight with that sword!" he cried. "Alas! Alas! Where is my magic sword, Excalibur?"

Then the beautiful lady laughed, put her hand behind her, and brought out what looked like Arthur's own sword, Excalibur! And the King, with great joy, took it into his hand and set off for the meadow, with all the twenty knights, pale and thin and trembling between hope and fear, walking two-and-two behind him.

This was, indeed, a great adventure—much greater than King Arthur knew. For the ship was a witch's ship, and the twelve dancing fairies were wicked fairies, and the lady who called herself the Princess of the Castle Perilous was the wickedest fairy of them all. Because, you must know, Morgan-le-Fey, Arthur's sister, had made herself Queen of the Water-Witches, and she wished her brother, the King, to be killed. So she had set all this magic afoot, and had also stolen Arthur's real sword, Excalibur, and given it to the knight who was waiting for the King in the meadow, prancing up and down over the daisies on his great, strong horse.

When he saw Arthur coming, he rode toward him with a great shout, waving the stolen Excalibur around and around his head. The King spurred his own horse forward, and the two met with a ringing crash of steel. Over and over again, they struck at each other, but King Arthur felt, with anguish, that his own sword was not striking keen and true. Then, even in the thick of the battle, he found time to gaze at the beautiful jewels in the scabbard of the sword that his enemy used so cleverly and well. And all at once, the King guessed that some terrible treachery was at work —that the other knight was fighting with the true

Excalibur, and that the sword in his own hands was not even made of fighting steel.

As Arthur realized this, he wavered in his saddle and almost fell. The wicked lord who fought him swung Excalibur high to strike the last blow. But at that very moment, the waters of the river which flowed round the meadow were suddenly and strangely disturbed. Out of the sparkling foam sprang a figure no less sparkling, and across the grass swept a beautiful lady, with dripping golden hair, and a long silver gown trailing yards behind her. It was the water-fairy who had brought up Sir Lancelot, and who had heard from the moor hens and little fishes of the plot made by Morgan-le-Fey, and was hurrying as fast as she could to the rescue.

She swept past the twenty pale knights and stood poised on her little white feet just above the grass, half-resting on the meadow flowers and half-hanging on her misty wings in the air. She waved her white hands and cried out magical words in a voice that was just like the bubbling of the brook. And the wicked lord on the big horse dropped Excalibur almost into Arthur's very hands! The King seized his own good sword again by its jeweled hilt and, with a shout of victory, stabbed his enemy through the breast. The big knight fell heavily to the ground and lay there, as nearly dead as possible.

His servants came running from the castle and

took him in. He got better in the end, but nobody cared much about that. What everybody did care about was that the twenty imprisoned knights were set free, and went joyfully home to their twenty faithful wives! The Lady of the Lake slid back into her shining, bubbling river; Arthur, carrying Excalibur, galloped off to Camelot; and as for the twelve wicked fairies, and the thirteenth who was the wickedest of all, no doubt they went on dancing forever on the little ship with the hundred torches and the embroidered silken sails.

They were only water-fairies, you see, and they had done what the Queen of the Water-Witches had ordered them to do. And, after all, it had been a right noble and fine adventure for King Arthur, and as he had come out of it victorious, he had no reason to complain.

Sir Lancelot of the Lake

A few chapters back you read about the baby Prince who was stolen by the water-fairy. He was very happy in the enchanted city at the bottom of the lake, the pet of all the water-fairies, but the very particular pet of the Queen, who would dance him in her arms, calling him "Son of a King." Little Lancelot would crow with delight and pat her beautiful green dress. In time, he grew into a tall and handsome youth. The Queen knew that she could not keep him with her forever, and so she put him in charge of a woodman who lived in the forest that grew all round the waters of the enchanted lake. Every morning the Lady of the Lake would take him up, up, up through the green waters, and set him upon the flowery bank, and call the woodman to come from his home and lead the boy into the forest to spend the day. But because the lake was a part of Fairyland, Lancelot never knew that the fine city where he lived was really beneath the water. He imagined that he just walked out of it into the forest through the mists of the morning, and returned to it at night through the moonlight and falling dew. But the lady whom he loved like his own mother always stood on the edge of the morning mist to wave him forward, and waited under the moonbeams, in the evening, to welcome him home.

In the forest the woodman taught him all the craft of a huntsman: the way to find the little brown hares, the wild foxes, the great strong-tusked boars, and the beautiful antlered deer. Lancelot grew clever and strong in his happy woodland life. He could shoot an arrow straight and true, shoe and saddle a horse, and climb the crags as high as the eagle's nest. How wonderful life seemed to him lived as the forest people lived it! How firm his muscle grew, how bright his young eyes, how vigorous and alert his frame! All day he was on foot, or a-horse, upon the hills or among the trees. At night, as he slept in his home in the enchanted city under the lake, he dreamed of doing noble deeds when he was a man.

Then, one day, as he hunted with the forest people, he heard them talking of a great King who was named Arthur, and who was the head of a gallant company of gentlemen who called themselves the knights of the Round Table. Wonderful stories were told of these knights—of their courage, their beauty, and their pride. All that night Lancelot lay awake, thinking about Arthur; and the next morning, as the sweet water-fairy led him to the misty horizon that lay beyond the en-

Sir Lancelot of the Lake

chanted city, he told her of what he had heard, and said that nothing, nothing, could ever make him happy unless he were allowed to go to Arthur's court and become a knight of the Round Table.

"Son of a King," said the water-fairy, half sadly, half triumphantly, "I have guessed that this would be your destiny! I have known I could not keep you always, because you are—well, what you are! But can you be brave enough to join Arthur's knighthood! Can you take and keep the great Vow? Can you, forever, be courteous, without baseness, kind to all, pitiful to the sad, generous to the poor, stern to the guilty—and choose death, at any time, before dishonor?"

Lancelot cried out that, indeed, he could. He said that to join in the Vow was the only thing he wanted in the whole world. So then this Lady of the Lake bent her head and consented. And from that moment, the preparations for Lancelot's departure to Arthur's court began.

And such preparations they were! The waterfairy had a suit of armor made for him, all of silver and pearls. She gave him a sword, long and shining, and a white satin mantle, trimmed with ermine. Then she dressed herself, also, in a robe of gleaming white satin, with ermine and silver upon the sleeves and hem. She chose her prettiest maidens, and her sprightliest pages, and she brought her fairy horses out of their fairy stalls.

From the enchanted palace she took long rolls of silk, and she had the silk made into tents for shelter on the way. Then, with songs and music, the beautiful procession set off; they passed through the mists that lay on the borders of their Fairyland, and rode through the forests and meadows of West-over-the-Sea, on their way to the castle of Camelot.

Arthur was coming back from hunting when he saw this sparkling company which traveled toward him through the twilight, looking as if it were made of sea-foam and stars. Astonished, he drew in his horse and waited. Then, though he did not recognize her, the Lady of the Lake rode forward in advance of the rest, as softly as a pale moth might flit across the dusky grass. Behind the fairy rode young Lancelot, all silvery-white in his beautiful armor and royal mantle; so that, indeed, he seemed no less fairylike than the delicate, shimmering lady in front of him.

The fairy paused as she reached Arthur's side and looked very earnestly at the astonished King. Then she waved to Lancelot to draw near, also.

"Son of a King!" she said to Arthur. "I have brought you a good knight and true. He, also, is the son of a King. Admit him to your fellowship, I pray you, and make him a knight of the Round Table."

Arthur turned in his saddle and fixed his eyes

gravely upon the youth in the white, shining armor, who rode up to the side of the lady.

"He is only a boy," said the King. "Is he ready to prove himself? Has he done battle yet in any just cause? Has he suffered for the sake of the weak, protected the innocent, or punished the guilty?"

"Not yet," answered the fairy gently. "But it is his most earnest wish to do so."

Arthur turned to Sir Gawaine, who sat on his horse by the King's side.

"Take the boy to your chamber," said Arthur. "Let him watch by his armor tonight in the chapel by the castle. Then, tomorrow, bring him to me."

He saluted the fairy, still not recognizing this beautiful and gracious lady who had brought her son to be a knight of the Round Table. He had no idea, at the moment, that she was a fairy at all, the one who had saved him and was cousin to the very fairy who had stretched a white hand and arm out of the water to give him his sword, Excalibur. The lady bent from her white horse toward Lancelot, kissed him tenderly, and placed a ring from her own hand upon his finger.

"Take this ring," said she. "Wear it always in battle. If you are hard-pressed by an enemy, turn it upon your finger. It will make you invisible. Turn it again, and your armor will change color—

from silver to black, from black to green, from green again to silver. Good-bye, dear son of a King! Good-bye!"

She kissed him again and rode back to the white and starry company who waited for her in the gathering night. Then they all rode silently away, and the sparkle of them died out among the trees. But Lancelot, in his silver armor, followed the King, and Sir Gawaine, and all the rest of the knights, into the castle of Camelot.

Sir Gawaine took him to his chamber, gave him meat and wine, and set him to watch his armor in the chapel, which all those who desired knighthood had to do. The next day he took him to Arthur on his throne in the great hall. There, for the first time, Lancelot saw Guinevere, the Queen.

And when he saw her, her beauty and sweetness went through him like a flame. All unknown to her, he stooped and lifted up a little knot of flowers that she had dropped. That little knot of flowers he kept till the end of his life.

And now the tournament of the day was announced, and the King said that Lancelot might take his part in it. So the young Prince from the enchanted lake of Fairyland mounted his horse and rode with the other knights into the meadow, where, very soon, a great mock battle began.

How they wrestled, and fought, and clashed swords, and galloped their horses! It was one of the finest tournaments ever seen, and, very soon, all who were watching began to speak of the wonderful courage and cleverness of a young strange knight in silver armor that shone like sea foam and stars. But even while they were speaking, he disappeared and a black knight was seen in his place, looking like some strange figure carved in ebony. Then the black knight vanished in his turn, and a knight in green appeared, like some magician of the forest, fallen straight from the emerald heart of an oak. In another moment this knight of the woodlands was gone, and there was the silver knight again, flashing across the meadow like a beautiful comet! And so on, and so on, and so on! For the black knight, and the silver knight, and the knight in emerald green were, all and each of them, none other than Lancelot of the Lake, who was galloping all over the meadow, continually turning his magic ring!

At last, the great mock battle was over, and there was a great call for the silver knight, and the black knight, and the knight in emerald green. But only the silver knight came forward—and in his hand he held the trophies of all three!

The people who had watched the tournament knew that some fairy had been helping the silver knight in some mysterious way. So they were full of respect for him, and cried out that he must indeed be made a knight of the Round Table, drink the cup of fellowship, and join in the great Vow.

And the Queen smiled, as she looked on, while the King knighted him, and, in memory of the water-fairy, named him Sir Lancelot of the Lake.

Sir Lancelot, as he knelt before Arthur, felt all the love of his brave young spirit go out to the King and to his sweet lady, Guinevere. He remembered the little knot of flowers that he wore close to his heart, and he vowed to himself that all the rest of his life should be spent in the service of the Queen.

The Coming of Galahad

All the knights of the Round Table were at supper one evening when the adventure of Sir Galahad began. It began with a lady on a white horse, who rode in at the open doorway, calling for Sir Lancelot of the Lake. King Arthur pointed him out, and she beckoned to him with a queenly hand and told him to follow her. So away they rode into the forest, the lady in front and Sir Lancelot a little way behind.

She reminded him of his own fairy of long ago as she moved on, pale and beautiful, among the shadowy trees. Presently they came to a great building, and the lady dismounted and gave her horse to a page who hastened out to meet them. Sir Lancelot dismounted, too; and the lady waved him good-bye (he was almost sure, now, it was his own fairy) and disappeared into the building. Then, after a few moments, came a sound of singing, and a procession of women in white hoods swept out through the gates. In the middle of the procession walked a youth, slim, upright, and very fair.

"And who may you be?" asked Sir Lancelot, taking his hand.

The good women made answer for him. They all spoke together, and their voices rustled through the trees like a soft wind.

"His name is Galahad!" said they. "His mother, the Princess Elaine, gave him long ago into our care. We have brought him up among everything that is fair and innocent. He is as beautiful as the young thorn tree that grew from Joseph's staff, and as pure as the snow that lies on its branches on Christmas Day. Take him to Arthur's court and ask Sir Bors if he remembers the baby in the Castle of the Hidden Grail!"

Then Sir Lancelot looked at Galahad, and the boy met his glance with quiet, frank eyes. The good women said good-bye to him and, sighing a little, went back into the castle, two and two together. And all through the night, Sir Lancelot and Galahad rested under the forest trees. At dawn, Sir Lancelot drew his sword and made the youth a knight, under the shining of the morning star, saying:

"May you be good forever, Sir Galahad, for you are the most beautiful knight I have ever seen."

Sir Galahad lifted his face to the dawn and smiled. But when Sir Lancelot would have taken him straight to Camelot, he shook his head.

"Not yet," said he. "I will come at Whitsuntide."

So he went away through the brightening morn-

The Coming of Galahad

ing, and Sir Lancelot watched until he was out of sight. Then the older knight rode back to Arthur's court, reaching Camelot just as the evening shadows were falling and the knights were gathering together, as usual, about the Round Table.

Then, before they all sat down, the same thing happened that had happened at the King's wedding banquet many, many years ago. Every seat began to glow with letters of shining gold, which spelled out the name of the knight who always sat there. And upon the Seat Perilous the letters flamed brightest and purest of all. But they read differently from the old mysterious warning, and the knights and barons, reading, spoke to each other in grave whispers.

"The many, many years that Merlin told us were to pass before this seat might be filled have passed away."

King Arthur drew near and looked at the letters for a long, long time. He remembered many things that Merlin had told him before the great wizard fell asleep in Broceliande. At last, he turned to his own place at the Round Table.

"Cover the Seat Perilous with a silken covering," he commanded. "Let no one touch it, nor go too near. Something is about to happen to our great company that will be beautiful and strange."

Even as he spoke, a rider galloped up to the door and, springing from his horse, clanked in among the knights, crying breathlessly: "Sirs! Sirs! A great adventure is awaiting you all." When they asked what it was, he answered that on the waters of the river was floating a vast stone that looked like red marble, and that in it was stuck a fair rich sword, with a handle of precious stones. And where was the knight for whom the sword was intended if not among those who sat at the Round Table at Camelot?

Then all the knights, and the King, and the Queen went down to the river, and sure enough, there was the red stone floating, with the bright sword in the middle of it. Sir Lancelot, Sir Bors, Sir Geraint, Sir Gawaine, Sir Perceval, all tried to draw it out, but in vain. Even Sir Perceval failed. So they went back to the darkening banqueting hall, where they seemed to hear strange voices whispering about the doors and windows. These, as the company entered, closed of themselves. As they closed, a bright light, like a summer morning, filled the hall, and a smell of hawthorn blossoms drifted through it, with the song of merry birds. Then, before the knights had recovered from their wonder, they saw standing among them an old man with a long white beard who had two strange bright snakes twisting round his neck, and a harp in his hands. By his side stood Galahad, dressed all in crimson satin, with a mantle of ermine hanging from his shoulders, and an empty scabbard swinging at his side.

The old man stood close by the Seat Perilous, and now he raised the silken covering with his frail white hand. Then everybody saw that the golden letters had changed a third time. "This is the place of Sir Galahad, the High Prince," ran the beautiful writing. And the old man took Galahad's hand and drew him to the wonderful seat.

As the fair young knight took his place, a long murmur of admiration and gladness ran round the table, and King Arthur cried out:

"It is for Sir Galahad that the sword is waiting —the sword which is fastened to the red marble stone that floats upon the stream! Old man, you have Merlin's look—Merlin's long white beard— Merlin's wonderful wise eyes! Tell us, is not this so?"

The old man bowed his head, struck his harp, and began to sing. He sang the story of Joseph, of the Rich Fisher, of the Silver Table, and of the Shining Cup. He sang of all that the Round Table meant, and of the new adventure to which the knights must vow themselves from that day—an adventure, not of lovely ladies, nor cruel giants, nor strange fairy hunts, but a search, a quest, for the treasure which had once been hidden in the strange gray castle where Sir Galahad was born. This pure young knight—so sang the old man— was the first Knight of the Grail. Now all the other knights of the Round Table must follow in his steps. Only the pure, the true, the good could ever find the lost treasure. Sir Bors had had a glimpse of it—so, too, had Sir Perceval, Sir Lancelot, and others. But to Sir Galahad alone had it been a beautiful thing that was just part of his daily life.

All the time the old man sang, Sir Galahad sat quietly in the Seat Perilous, his hand on his empty scabbard. By and by, he rose, and went out of the banqueting hall, down to the river, which flowed black and silver through the night. The stone rocked softly on it, and the handle of the sword glowed above. Sir Galahad drew it from the red marble and went back.

Then the knights all sprang to their feet and acclaimed him, for they saw the fairy sword in his hand. As they shouted their joy in him, the hall went quite dark again, and everybody was, all at once, very quiet. For, among the shadows, a flame like the flame of a candle could be seen.

The slim flame grew and grew, until it became a great soft light. In the red heart of it moved a spirit who looked like the dumb maiden. She floated through the hall, and her feet made no sound. In her hands, she held aloft the Shining Cup of the Grail.

The vision lasted only a minute before it faded. Then everything was dark again. But, in the hush, the old man began to sing once more, and the moon, suddenly shining through the window, showed Sir Galahad, all in silver armor; the queer, bright snakes that twisted about the old minstrel's neck; and the great company of shadowy knights seated at the Round Table, listening to the Song of the Holy Grail.

The Passing of the King

Everything was different, somehow, at King Arthur's court since the coming of Sir Galahad. The knights were all vowed, now, to the search for the Holy Grail, which had disappeared from the castle of King Pelles when Sir Galahad went away. Who had taken it, everybody asked one another; but no one could give a reply. Had it really been carried through the banqueting hall the night that Sir Galahad had taken his place upon the Perilous Seat? Or was it only a dream, a vision, that the knights had seen? If it were a vision, would any of them see it again? They could not answer these questions; but, one and all, they sought for the Shining Cup for the rest of their lives.

Joseph and the Rich Fisher had long ago passed away, you see; and perhaps they alone knew what the Holy Grail really was. The strange old minstrel with the two bright snakes round his neck knew just a little, but not everything. He wore the snakes to show that he belonged to the old, old order of bards—the men who were something like priests and who sang stories of great nations and greater kings. His Song of the Holy Grail was written down in the little book that he must have found in Merlin's mysterious house with the seventy windows and the sixty doors. For Merlin was one of these bards himself, and very likely wore bright snakes about his neck as he came and went at King Arthur's court, though we are not exactly told that he ever did. But then, we are by no means told all that happened in those days, and if we were, perhaps we should not believe it. This we do know, however: that all the knights who searched for the lost Grail Cup knew that they had no chance of finding it, or even catching a glimpse of it in a vision, unless they were perfectly good and true and pure and without reproach. So all of them tried hard to be so; and though none of them ever quite succeeded, the very trying made their lives beautiful—just as shining and beautiful as the silver armor they wore, and the spears and swords that they carried in their hands.

They still met at the Round Table, still passed the Cup of Fellowship from hand to hand, but the King, as he sat among them, felt that he was growing old. His eyes were heavy, often, and his feet and hands were tired. And one day he was obliged to go into battle against an enemy when he was too weary to fight. He was struck down and wounded, and his faithful knights carried him to

The Passing of the King

a quiet, grassy place in a meadow, near which rippled the shining waters of a great lake.

King Arthur lay on the moss with his fingers on the handle of his sword Excalibur, and his followers stood around him with sad faces, for they thought that Death was about to take their beloved King. But he himself knew better. He smiled as he lay there, and his face was very bright. Lifting himself up a little, he looked toward the waters of the lake, and then he beckoned to a knight who was called Sir Bedivere.

"Take my sword Excalibur," said he. "Throw it as far as you can fling it toward the center of the lake. Then come back and tell me what happens."

Sir Bedivere took the sword and carried it to the edge of the lake. Night was falling and the moon was brightening above the quiet hills. In the moonlight, the jewels in the handle of Excalibur looked very rich and beautiful—so rich and so beautiful that Sir Bedivere felt he could not bear to throw the sword into the water. He hid it all among the forget-me-nots and meadowsweet, and went, empty-handed, back to the King.

"Did you throw the sword into the lake?" asked Arthur eagerly.

"Yes, sire," answered Sir Bedivere boldly.

"What happened?"

"Nothing happened, sire!"

The King lay back again with a groan.

"Faithless messenger!" he said. "You have not thrown the sword! Go! Do as I command."

Again, Sir Bedivere went, but again the beauty of Excalibur overcame him. He returned to the King and declared that he had flung the sword into the water, but still nothing had happened.

Arthur looked at him steadily, and his eyes made Sir Bedivere afraid.

"You are not speaking the truth!" cried the King. "Go! Do as I command!"

His voice was very strong and stern, and at last, Bedivere obeyed. Hurrying to the water's edge, he took Excalibur in his hand again, without daring to look at its beauty. The rubies and sapphires and diamonds of the handle flashed as he flung it far, far into the lake. Just as it was about to strike the water, a white hand and arm, clothed in a shining sleeve, rose above the ripples, and the outstretched fingers caught the sword by the hilt. Three times the hand waved Excalibur in the moonlight—then both arm and sword disappeared below the water, and all was still.

Breathless and awed, Sir Bedivere went back to the King and told what he had seen.

"It is well!" said Arthur. "Carry me to the lake!"

So his knights lifted him and carried him gently across the moonlit grass until they came to the water's edge. As they walked in slow procession, they saw a dim ship, like a dark barge, com-

ing from the middle of the lake toward the bank. Many ladies, shadowy in the pale light, were seated in it, with their heads bowed upon their hands. All of them were hooded; and three, who wore crowns upon their heads, looked like Queens.

Then the King bade the knights lay him in the barge, and they did so, and gave him into the care of the three Queens. Down from the hills swept a great wind—and it seemed as if the sound of sobbing and wailing was in its cold breath. The clouds rushed across the moon and the water of the lake looked black and terrible as the barge began to move away from the land. The knights stood upon the bank and watched as if they were in a dream.

Then, even as they watched, the darkness went away. Far, far off, right away as it were, beyond the mere, little shining islands began to show, bright and beautiful and for all the world like sunset clouds. All the knights had heard of these islands, and knew that they were called the Isles of the Blest. In the very center of them was the fairest of all, named Avalon. Its valleys were fragrant with flowers, and in its orchard grew trees that bore golden apples. It seemed to the knights that the barge with the three fairy Queens and the weary human King sailed right up to the shores of Avalon, and that a number of bright and beautiful people came to meet it. Then the whole vision faded. Nothing was left but the lake, and

The Passing of the King

the moonlit meadows, and the memory of the great and only King of the Round Table.

But some people say that Arthur lives and is happy in Avalon to this day, and that there he has met Joseph, and the Rich Fisher, and his wise old teacher, Merlin, the great magician. They say, too, that it is in Avalon that the Silver Table is hidden, on which stands the Shining Cup; and that the mysterious feast is held there every evening, which fills all the guests with joy and amazement, just as they were filled with joy and amazement hundreds of years ago on that Christmas Day when Joseph's staff broke into blossom at Glastonbury.

OTHER AIRMONT CLASSICS

Complete and Unabridged with Introductions

CL 1	PRIDE AND PREJUDICE,	*Jane Austen*
CL 2	TREASURE ISLAND,	*Robert Louis Stevenson*
CL 3	THE RED BADGE OF COURAGE,	*Stephen Crane*
CL 4	HUCKLEBERRY FINN,	*Mark Twain*
CL 5	THE LAST OF THE MOHICANS,	*Cooper*
CL 6	TOM SAWYER,	*Mark Twain*
CL 7	THE SCARLET LETTER,	*Nathaniel Hawthorne*
CL 8	EDGAR ALLAN POE,	*Selected Stories and Poems*
CL 9	OLIVER TWIST,	*Charles Dickens*
CL10	KIDNAPPED,	*Robert Louis Stevenson*
CL11	WUTHERING HEIGHTS,	*Emily Brontë*
CL12	20,000 LEAGUES UNDER THE SEA,	*Jules Verne*
CL13	THE SWISS FAMILY ROBINSON,	*Johann Wyss*
CL14	SILAS MARNER,	*George Eliot*
CL15	GULLIVER'S TRAVELS,	*Jonathan Swift*
CL16	THE HOUSE OF THE SEVEN GABLES,	*Hawthorne*
CL17	JANE EYRE,	*Charlotte Brontë*
CL18	HEIDI,	*Johanna Spyri*
CL19	FRANKENSTEIN,	*Mary Shelley*
CL20	THE BLACK ARROW,	*Robert Louis Stevenson*
CL21	A TALE OF TWO CITIES,	*Charles Dickens*
CL22	ROBINSON CRUSOE,	*Daniel DeFoe*
CL23	BLACK BEAUTY,	*Anna Sewell*
CL24	AROUND THE WORLD IN 80 DAYS,	*Jules Verne*
CL25	O. HENRY,	*The Four Million and other stories*
CL26	A CHRISTMAS CAROL,	*Charles Dickens*
CL27	CAPTAINS COURAGEOUS,	*Rudyard Kipling*
CL28	THE SCARLET PIMPERNEL,	*Baroness Orczy*
CL29	A CONNECTICUT YANKEE,	*Twain*
CL30	CALL OF THE WILD,	*Jack London*
CL31	THE DEERSLAYER,	*James Fenimore Cooper*
CL32	THE PRINCE AND THE PAUPER,	*Mark Twain*
CL33	MOBY DICK,	*Herman Melville*
CL34	IVANHOE,	*Sir Walter Scott*
CL35	THE PATHFINDER,	*James Fenimore Cooper*
CL36	WHITE FANG,	*Jack London*
CL37	THE OREGON TRAIL,	*Francis Parkman*
CL38	THE RETURN OF THE NATIVE,	*Thomas Hardy*
CL39	THE PICTURE OF DORIAN GRAY,	*Oscar Wilde*
CL40	THE INVISIBLE MAN,	*H. G. Wells*
CL41	THE PRAIRIE,	*Cooper*
CL42	DR. JEKYLL AND MR. HYDE,	*Stevenson*
CL43	THE MILL ON THE FLOSS,	*George Eliot*
CL44	THE TIME MACHINE,	*H. G. Wells*
CL45	THE WAR OF THE WORLDS,	*H. G. Wells*
CL46	THE VIRGINIAN,	*Owen Wister*
CL47	THE MASTER OF BALLANTRAE,	*Stevenson*
CL48	MICHAEL STROGOFF,	*Jules Verne*
CL49	THE PIONEERS,	*James Fenimore Cooper*
CL50	THE LEGEND OF SLEEPY HOLLOW,	*Irving*
CL51	THE OUTCASTS OF POKER FLAT,	*Bret Harte*
CL52	THE VICAR OF WAKEFIELD,	*Oliver Goldsmith*
CL53	TYPEE,	*Herman Melville*
CL54	LORD JIM,	*Joseph Conrad*
CL55	LIFE ON THE MISSISSIPPI,	*Mark Twain*
CL56	THE PRINCE,	*Niccoló Machiavelli*
CL57	THE ODYSSEY,	*Homer*
CL58	SENSE AND SENSIBILITY,	*Jane Austen*
CL59	THE FOOD OF THE GODS,	*H. G. Wells*

- CL60 A JOURNEY TO THE CENTER OF THE EARTH, *Verne*
- CL61 THE AGE OF CHIVALRY, *Thomas Bulfinch*
- CL62 THE HOUND OF THE BASKERVILLES, *Doyle*
- CL63 THE MAYOR OF CASTERBRIDGE, *Thomas Hardy*
- CL64 THE SEA WOLF, *Jack London*
- CL65 DAVID COPPERFIELD, *Charles Dickens*
- CL66 TWICE-TOLD TALES, *Nathaniel Hawthorne*
- CL67 ROBIN HOOD
- CL68 GREAT EXPECTATIONS, *Charles Dickens*
- CL69 THE WIZARD OF OZ, *L. Frank Baum*
- CL70 THE STORY OF MY LIFE, *Helen Keller*
- CL71 THE AUTOBIOGRAPHY OF BENJAMIN FRANKLIN
- CL72 DRACULA, *Bram Stoker*
- CL73 MASTER OF THE WORLD, *Jules Verne*
- CL74 BEN HUR, *Lew Wallace*
- CL75 KIM, *Rudyard Kipling*
- CL76 THE MOONSTONE, *William Wilkie Collins*
- CL77 THE MYSTERIOUS ISLAND, *Jules Verne*
- CL78 THE FIRST MEN IN THE MOON, *H. G. Wells*
- CL79 ALICE'S ADVENTURES IN WONDERLAND, *L. Carroll*
- CL80 THE AGE OF FABLE, *Thomas Bulfinch*
- CL81 AESOP'S FABLES
- CL82 TESS OF THE D'URBERVILLES, *Thomas Hardy*
- CL83 WALDEN—ESSAY ON CIVIL DISOBEDIENCE, *Thoreau*
- CL84 PÈRE GORIOT, *Honoré de Balzac*
- CL85 TWO YEARS BEFORE THE MAST, *Charles Henry Dana*
- CL86 THE JUNGLE, *Upton Sinclair*
- CL87 GREEN MANSIONS, *W. H. Hudson*
- CL88 THE MUTINY ON BOARD H.M.S. BOUNTY, *Wm. Bligh*
- CL89 MADAME BOVARY, *Gustave Flaubert*
- CL90 THE WAY OF ALL FLESH, *Samuel Butler*
- CL91 LEAVES OF GRASS, *Walt Whitman*
- CL92 MASTER SKYLARK, *John Bennett*
- CL93 MEN OF IRON, *Howard Pyle*
- CL94 EVANGELINE and other poems, *Henry W. Longfellow*
- CL95 THE AMBASSADORS, *Henry James*
- CL96 MAN AND SUPERMAN, *George Bernard Shaw*
- CL97 THE ADVENTURES OF SHERLOCK HOLMES, *Doyle*
- CL98 THE PORTRAIT OF A LADY, *Henry James*
- CL99 HANS BRINKER; OR, THE SILVER SKATES, *Mary Mapes Dodge*
- CL100 AT THE BACK OF THE NORTH WIND, *George Macdonald*
- CL101 THE ADVENTURES OF PINOCCHIO, *Carlo Collodi*
- CL102 EMMA, *Jane Austen*
- CL103 ADAM BEDE, *George Eliot*
- CL104 THE MARBLE FAUN, *Nathaniel Hawthorne*
- CL105 THE WIND IN THE WILLOWS, *Kenneth Grahame*
- CL106 LITTLE WOMEN, *Louisa May Alcott*
- CL107 PERSUASION, *Jane Austen*
- CL108 JUDE THE OBSCURE, *Thomas Hardy*
- CL109 THE JUNGLE BOOKS, *Rudyard Kipling*
- CL110 THE ISLAND OF DR. MOREAU, *H. G. Wells*
- CL111 IN THE DAYS OF THE COMET, *H. G. Wells*
- CL112 HEART OF DARKNESS and THE END OF THE TETHER, *Joseph Conrad*
- CL113 AN OUTCAST OF THE ISLANDS, *Joseph Conrad*
- CL114 THE MYSTERY OF EDWIN DROOD, *Charles Dickens*
- CL115 THE ILLIAD, *Homer*
- CL116 BILLY BUDD AND THE ENCANTADAS, *H. Melville*
- CL117 CANDIDE AND ZADIG, *Voltaire*
- CL118 A WONDER BOOK, *Nathaniel Hawthorne*
- CL119 CAESAR AND CLEOPATRA, *George Bernard Shaw*

CL120	FOUR MAJOR PLAYS, *Henrik Ibsen*
CL121	THE CONFIDENCE MAN, *Herman Melville*
CL122	DEAD SOULS, *Nikolai Gogol*
CL123	JUST SO STORIES, *Rudyard Kipling*
CL124	PUDD'NHEAD WILSON, *Mark Twain*
CL125	ANNA KARENINA, *Leo Tolstoy*
CL126	TOM SAWYER ABROAD and TOM SAWYER, DETECTIVE, *Mark Twain*
CL127	THE THREE MUSKETEERS, *Alexandre Dumas*
CL128	THE BROTHERS KARAMAZOV, *Fyodor Dostoyevsky*
CL129	FATHERS AND SONS, *Ivan Turgenev*
CL130	EREWHON, *Samuel Butler*
CL131	MANSFIELD PARK, *Jane Austen*
CL132	QUENTIN DURWARD, *Sir Walter Scott*
CL133	PEER GYNT, *Henrik Ibsen*
CL134	ROUGHING IT, *Mark Twain*
CL135	TOM JONES, *Henry Fielding*
CL136	FAR FROM THE MADDING CROWD, *Thomas Hardy*
CL137	THE LADY OF THE LAKE, *Sir Walter Scott*
CL138	VANITY FAIR, *William M. Thackeray*
CL139	THE PRISONER OF ZENDA, *Anthony Hope*
CL140	KING SOLOMON'S MINES, *H. Rider Haggard*
CL141	BOB, SON OF BATTLE, *Alfred Ollivant*
CL142	FROM THE EARTH TO THE MOON, *Jules Verne*
CL143	UNCLE TOM'S CABIN, *Harriet B. Stowe*
CL144	REBECCA OF SUNNYBROOK FARM, *Kate D. Wiggin*
CL145	CRIME AND PUNISHMENT, *Fyodor Dostoyevsky*
CL146	SHE, *H. Rider Haggard*
CL147	SISTER CARRIE, *Theodore Dreiser*
CL148	JANICE MEREDITH, *Paul L. Ford*
CL149	LORNA DOONE, *Richard D. Blackmore*
CL150	THE MAN IN THE IRON MASK, *Alexandre Dumas*
CL151	THE INNOCENTS ABROAD, *Mark Twain*
CL152	TRISTRAM SHANDY, *Lawrence Sterne*
CL153	DON QUIXOTE, *Miguel de Cervantes*
CL154	THE COUNT OF MONTE CRISTO, *Alexandre Dumas*
CL155	THE TURN OF THE SCREW, *Henry James*
CL156	THE PRINCESS AND THE GOBLIN, *G. Macdonald*
CL157	UP FROM SLAVERY, *Booker T. Washington*
CL158	MONSIEUR BEAUCAIRE and THE BEAUTIFUL LADY, *Booth Tarkington*
CL159	THE AUTOCRAT OF THE BREAKFAST-TABLE, *Oliver Wendell Holmes*
CL160	TO HAVE AND TO HOLD, *Mary Johnston*
CL161	THE BEST SHORT STORIES OF GUY DE MAUPASSANT
CL162	THE HUNCHBACK OF NOTRE-DAME, *Victor Hugo*
CL163	THE LADY OR THE TIGER, *Frank Stockton*
CL164	DEMOCRACY, AN AMERICAN NOVEL, *H. Adams*
CL165	THE RISE OF SILAS LAPHAM, *William D. Howells*
CL166	MAGGIE AND OTHER STORIES, *Stephen Crane*
CL167	STORIES OF KING ARTHUR, *Winder*
CL168	GRIMM'S FAIRY TALES
CL169	HANS CHRISTIAN ANDERSEN'S FAIRY TALES
CL170	A STORY OF THE RED CROSS, *Clara Barton*
CL171	SHORT STORIES OF MARK TWAIN, *Mark Twain*
CL172	PLATO'S REPUBLIC, *Jowett Translation*
CL173	PARADISE LOST and PARADISE REGAINED, *Milton*
CL174	TOM BROWN'S SCHOOL DAYS, *Thomas Hughes*
CL175	TANGLEWOOD TALES, *Nathaniel Hawthorne*
CL176	THE AMERICAN, *Henry James*
CL177	VIRGIL'S AENEID, *Dryden's Translation*